How To Be Happy

and

Positive II

Living A Life Of Peace and Harmony

Table of Contents

Introduction 1

Chapter 1: The Power Of Happiness and Positivity 3

Chapter 2: How To Be The Best We Can Be 11

Chapter 3: The Unhinged Soul 24

Chapter 4: Happiness In Our Everyday Lives 32

Chapter 5: How To Escape The World of Negativity 43

Chapter 6: Perspective Is The Key To A Healthy State Of Mind 53

Chapter 7: Live With The Notion Of Selflessness 62

Chapter 8: The Beauty of Being You 71

Chapter 9: Eliminate Traumas and Fears in Your Life 82

Chapter 10: Gain A Greater Awareness Of Yourself And Others 100

Chapter 11: Achieve The Success That You Deserve 106

Introduction

Are you a happy person deep inside? Do you strive to be happy and live your life to the fullest and fulfill all your dreams, hopes and desires. Look no further because you'll be able to exist in a state of purity and bliss after learning the principles in this book and reading. Happiness is only a state of mind, a way of living, and a presence of being and fulfilling your life's dreams, goals and desires. Being a positive person and living a daily life of bliss and joy isn't always something that comes easily, it often takes various forms of practice to be able to achieve this state of nirvana and good within yourself. Many people strive to live a happy and fulfilled life but aren't always able to do so due to issues with their inner selves, a negative past, a history of negative experiences, or other various factors that apply to affecting a person's personal life and situation. People often smile in haste and wish their lives were fuller and with more joy, love, peace and true jubilation within. Being a positive person and living your life in the format of love and truth can happen with learning how to access these feelings and this state of bliss energy and transforming negative ideations and thoughtforms into positive ones.

If you truly want to be fulfilled within your heart and life, you have to learn to look deep within yourself, analyze and examine who you are, and learn about yourself and gain a greater awareness of your own intents and desires in life.

Do you wish to do more in life or grow into a greater person than you are? Or are you alright with being in the position you are currently? Many people tend to not examine this particular given situation. They aren't sure where they are with their places in life, and sometimes may wonder if they should be doing more or should be fulfilling their goals and desires somehow. Others may not have any thoughts as to what they should be doing or where they are in their current place in life. If you want to do more in life, then you'll have to take chances and step out of the box you've placed yourself in and try your hardest to fulfill bucket list items and other scenarios that you've been too afraid or busy to try.

Chapter 1

The Power Of Happiness and Positivity

Happiness is the joy we exist in and the life we seek to live in without the hassles of states of evil, confusion hate angst and other emotions.

The happiness and joy we so seek and desire in our worlds and universe is right at the grasp of our fingertips. It is right underneath our breath and fully accessible in every area we desire if we only know how to utilize and attain its benefits. We can grasp the positivity from every area in our world along with nature and within everything surrounding us. Happiness is within us and amongst us and we just need to know how to grasp and use it in order to bless our lives and those of others.

Doing good to others. Selfless love and goodness and the desire to do good, spread it and the desire to harness good for others and want good for others. Happiness entails selfless love and pure positive energy that exists within a world of unlimited bliss and freedom from negativity and darkness. Once we are fortunate enough to obtain this bliss learn of it acknowledge all that it is and how it is present in our world, we are able to gain access to utilizing it within our lives and allowing it to spread and create beauty and good within and a life of abundance and joy and nothing else.

Happiness is the bountiful source of love that radiates deep within our spirits and beings and allows us to flourish within the definition of hope and freedom. We exist in a confusing world where selfishness reigns and there are aspects in this world where harmony and peace seem to be non-existent. We want to exist in a reality where goodness is the norm and there is an abundance of pure positive energy and goodness anywhere we journey and within our realities and so we can create this positivity and joy and focus on allowing it to become greater and more widespread

The state of being happy and mindful lies within a person's current state of being and the experiences they've come across and how they react to these stimuli and how they live their life and how their perceptions shape their reality.

Harnessing positive power is one of the most important feats of being able to exist within an eclectic reality of peace and prosperity. If we harness the positive power we hold within ourselves, we can exercise our right to live in a constant state of love and harmony

We can harness unlimited happiness and abundance In our lives if we choose to do so by practicing the art of exercising love and positivity in our lives within every aspect of our beings. There is no limit to the amount of happiness and love we possess and that can be manifested in our world once the skyballing effects of positivity begin to occur in our reality.

The happiness and joy we so seek and desire in our worlds and universe is right at the grasp of our fingertips. It is right underneath our breath and fully accessible in every area we desire if we only know how to utilize and attain its benefits. We can grasp the positivity from every area in our world along with nature and within everything surrounding us. Happiness is within us and amongst us and we just need to know how to grasp and use it in order to bless our lives and those of others.

I am a happy joyous person and seek to live this fulfilled beautiful joyous wondrous life with my own given self in a state of being present happy and conscious and always being aware of my presence and in my present self regardless of anything that affects or surrounds me. I am engulfed with happiness and pleasure always and will always live in this state while those negative things happening to me become lesser in the background and wither away slowly. They become whispers and less important than the happiness and positivity that has taken over and become a part of my very being.

Doing good to others. Selfless love and goodness and the desire to do good, spread it and the desire to harness good for others and want good for others. Happiness entails selfless love and pure positive energy that exists within a world of unlimited bliss and freedom from negativity and darkness. Once we are fortunate enough to obtain this bliss learn of it acknowledge all that it is and how it is present in our world, we are able to gain access to utilizing it within our lives and allowing it to spread and create beauty and good within and a life of abundance and joy and nothing else.

Manifestation can occur due to being able to grasp the concept that what we think and feel and project out into the world and our realities has the power and ability to create experiences and scenarios and create forms of our reality in order to allow us to live within the reality that we create for ourselves and lets us be the creator of our destiny.

The collective perspective of being able to exist in a world of happiness and bliss can contribute to growing in goodness and nature and enhance the experiences of positivity and harmony in little experiences in life.

The harmony within our presence can create greater excursions and experiences and allow for a more well rounded experience in a world of truth and jubilation.

The Power of Positivity

The power of positivity is the most encapsulating means for someone to be a happy and positive person full of only goodness and love and can assist someone in reaching new heights when it comes to being happy and elated in general. The power of goodness allows us to become better people and beacons towards others and guide others towards doing better deeds and living better lives in a harmonious nature with others. We need to live in a world where we use our gifts and talents to aid others in doing great and good things and doing these great things ourselves.

How can we be more positive minded people and how can we become beacons of those who strive to be more positive? It's important to live a life and lifestyle that supports us when it comes to being at our highest success. We can focus on the good things in our lives and what matters and accept and appreciate all that exists in our lives and world.

Positivity should be a part of our everyday world, and we need to practice various forms of increasing our positive attributes and utilizing any good benefits that exist within our life.

The beauty of love and truth allows for the greater collective good within a person's life, and being in a state of love and wanting to spread and speak truth allows a person to generate more goodness and good energy. The better energy you generate and the more good deeds and qualities you relish in, the more you create positive harmonious beautiful pure energies within yourself and surrounding you and in your life. These energies become a part of your soul, spirit and being and spread to other parts of your life and world creating an effect of more positivity coming your way.

Give out positive energy

The importance of being kind. Be positive. When you give out positive energy, it comes back to you tenfold, and this is the secret to remaining positive and happy. Continue giving out positive energy, because the more you give out, the more that comes back to you. Most people aren't aware of this concept, yet it is the truth. Giving out positive energy creates a whirlwind of goodness and energy that's being unleashed coming back onto you in excess forms and with force.

Giving is a form of creating large amounts of positive and good energies and once you go through the process and cycle of giving energy out to others or giving anything to others, it will create a pattern of good coming back to the sender and the person committing these very actions. Positive energy is extremely contagious and will come back tenfold to those who give it out. The same works with negative energy.

Healing begins in the mind and makes its way to hundreds of points in the body and downward.

Being positive isn't just a mindset. It's meant to be a conscious way of life and it's important to live this way of life in everything that we think, do and believe in.

The key to happiness is the concept of fulfillment and believing in yourself and knowing and feeling that sense of feeling as if you've accomplished a ton of different things within your special and blessed life.

We all feel as if we are happy and decent people, but the truth is that we have no clue how we truly feel inside and who we really are. This is the reality of many people's situation. We truly don't know how to feel deep within and we aren't sure what we're harnessing inwards and within, yet we tend to believe in and feel as if we've accomplished many things in life when sometimes those accomplishments just aren't enough for us. We strive for more and we strive to do better and yearn to be greater in each thing we do in every aspect of our life.

The key to happiness is the truthful and bliss of knowing that we have successfully strived to do extremely well within the confines of our thought and belief system and that we are successful and capable people who've handled our life situation very well.

Happiness is the key within us to attempt to learn how to live and harness our lives within the vast grips of confusion many people face on a daily basis. It allows us to live our life and be the true good we were meant to be rather than the meandering souls we may have become. It's important to focus on being a truly happy person within our souls and minds first and within our everyday lives, rather than being those who have become engulfed in a negative or downward spiral way of thinking and beliefs.

Happiness is a beautiful part of our souls, and we all strive to live in a world where we exist, where we can be in peace and our souls can have joy and harmony.

Happiness is a harmonious love you exhibit and find within yourself and your world and it's an important part of your life and bring to feel elated and joyful at all given times within your beautiful wonderful and special life. Your life matters and is of extreme importance and you deserve to feel constant happiness in it, not anger sadness grief or any negative emotions or feelings.

If you're ever negative or in a state of sadness or sorrow, it's imperative that you focus on trying to remove those negative parts of yourself and refreshing your positive ideations by living in the moment and really pushing good feelings into yourself and being the best person you can ever be.

Chapter 2

How To Be
The Best We Can Be

It's important to understand that this world and life are a gift that have been bestowed upon us, and that we need to utilize this gift with the greatest concept of gratefulness and appreciation that we can imagine. We are not on this planet by chance, and this beautiful gift has been given to us to allow us to experience the joys of being alive, living and experiencing the many wonders of being on this planet. Living on this planet should be a journey, and a momentary blessing that we should bask in and enjoy for all the beautiful pleasures that are given our way. Many people take for granted all the blessings they are allowed and blessed with and tend to perceive their life in negative terms and beliefs. The world is an oyster, and we are in it to explore, experience and journey, appreciate, not negate, fear, put down, abuse, or live in a negative or confused, angry unappreciative state of mind. We deserve to live within our world in a state of goodness and bliss rather than anger, confusion, lack of awareness or hate lingering within us. We deserve to be the best people that we can be, and this is something that a person can achieve and live by and within, rather than wondering what it's like to be happy or feel good within themselves.

Being in a state of harmony rather than fear

It's imperative to exist in a state of harmony, bliss, and love always in a given moment in a person's life rather than living in a state of fear, anger or lack of hope. This might not be an easy concept to master for most people. People lack a general awareness of their emotions within their world and life and are unaware of how or why they're feeling or why they're behaving and reacting towards stimuli the way they do. That's because people don't possess a higher awareness of their beliefs, ideas, emotions, and tend to not have a full understanding of the importance of having this concept of greater awareness. It can assist a person with understanding their own emotions, reactions and beliefs and allow them to know their own selves and others better. Existing in a state of harmony and joy with positive beliefs and thoughts can assist a person with gaining a far greater understanding of true inner happiness and can cultivate the notion of building upon those beliefs, values, feelings and can escalate those feelings of happiness and good within a person's body, mind and soul.

Loving every moment we live in

We must love each and every moment we live and exist in and every experience we undergo and partake in. For life again is a blessing and a world and venue gifted to us so we can enjoy our stay on this planet and enjoy being gifted with these experiences and evolve into greater and more harmonious and happy people and beings rather than exist in a world of hate, fear, negativity and anger. It is important to be happy about each and every moment we partake and exist in and find good, love and happiness within each and every moment in order to experience a constant state of happiness and true pleasure within ourselves.

Building upon positivity and good

One of the keys to happiness and inner peace is by building upon any and all positivity and good in your life, for positivity is very contagious and secretly will harness more and more good and positivity coming your way energetically and in other forms. If you truly want to live a life of good and happiness, then do more positive deeds, actions and have more positive thoughts, because more positive ideations, events and actions will come back to your world and to you in varying manners. This doesn't mean that negative events or outcomes can't occur in life either, because sometimes these events are inevitable as well through other people's actions or circumstances that seem out of our control. It's important however to eliminate those negative people or the source of this negativity in a person's life otherwise sometimes those kinds of people or situations just will not improve or and might even get worse and have a tremendous effect in a person's life. It's a good idea to send out positive thoughts, beliefs consistently, and constantly be kind towards others for that positivity will come right back to a person and allow a person to experience good and happiness every moment of their life and existence and will generally snowball into greater outcomes of good energy and true bliss for a person.

Focusing on the positive and fruitful aspects of our experiences. We should live our lives through the notion and lens of being happy and joyous and witnessing and experiencing the positive and good aspects of the endeavors we partake in. It's of immense importance to focus on the greater aspects of any event we partake and to take from these scenarios and situations that which is of benefit to us and to others. The more we focus on the positive within our world and experiences, the more positive experiences will flow towards us and within our lives in order to nourish and sustain our souls and beings.

Eliminating all negative ideas, beliefs, and thoughts

Our ideas and thoughts are a huge part of our world. Negative thoughtforms can take over our ways of thinking and cause us to exist in a state of fear, lack of harmony, hatred, anger and other lower emotions. We must eliminate all negative ideas and thoughts from our ways of thinking and our minds. We exist in a paradigm that is full of a plethora of varying interconnected thoughts, patterns, and forms. Our thoughts can control our reality and interfere in our life and sometimes cause negative events or experiences to take place. We have to exist in a scenario of thinking positive thoughts at all times and focus on being positive and believing in our own ideas and feelings.

Our feelings and ideas matter and are of extreme importance. Sometimes in life, people tend to stop believing in their own beliefs, and perceptions due to circumstances that have occurred in their world, past situations, negative people or other things in life.

We must learn to believe in our own feelings, ideas, thoughts and perspectives and not allow other people's negativity to get to us or bring us down. It's imperative to focus on our feelings, beliefs, and ideals rather than allowing others to have an impact on us. Once we've gained enough confidence and belief in our own feelings and thoughts, we will have built a stronghold for us to not stray from our true ideations, and this in turn will allow this to become the pillar of our belief systems, our thoughts and the perspectives we have about ourselves. We need to truly learn to appreciate, love and believe in the ideations we feel or believe in, rather than allowing other's perspectives or beliefs about ourselves or other things in life affect us. We should only allow our own perspectives to affect us, not other people's.

Gaining confidence in our world

Gaining confidence in your world is of utmost importance. You'll want to use methods to try to increase your confidence levels in general which involves focusing on the aspects which affect your self-esteem and examining what makes you feel a specific way and listing these things down.

In order to better your confidence levels you'll need to write down the things that you feel might bring you down or affect you negatively or that which makes you feel lesser or inferior. Once you write these aspects down, you can better understand and organize the concepts that you feel or are unsure of and that negatively hinder your life, you and aspects in your world.

Your self-esteem can sometimes be very shattered or have problems due to past experiences, traumas and other issues in life. It's important to remind yourself a lot of the time that you are a good and worthy person and that your opinions are important and that you matter. You also will need to do well at the things you do in order to build upon your internal confidence.

Confidence is something that is important for a person to have in their everyday lives. It allows them to feel secure in what they do in life and lets a person utilize their opinions and needs and exert who they are and not feel lesser in any way.

To grow your confidence levels you will need to focus on building up your self-esteem and creating ways of doing this using positive affirmations, internal ways of feeling confident and by focusing your attention on the great attributes you do possess

Believing in yourself and your beliefs, opinions and each and every aspect you carry and hold in your thoughts and being is one way of developing and creating greater confidence levels in yourself. You are an extremely important person and your values and beliefs matter.

Focus on bringing up your self-esteem by giving yourself positive ideas about yourself, loving yourself unconditionally and loving every aspect of yourself and who you are. Be good at the things you do for being successful and doing well will increase your confidence levels tenfold and allow the effects to snowball and grow into a greater and stronger person internally. If you're a sales person then sound stronger and more confident, learn new strategies for selling and become better at your position for that form of confidence will in fact seep into your everyday life and allow you to become confident in other venues as well.

You are an extremely confident, beautiful charismatic person who deserves the best things in life and in order for you to build on your confidence will need to focus on the positive things you possess and feed yourself with these positive attributes and understand that what you think or feel holds value and that you should be allowed to assert your opinions and yourself to others.

Support yourself and your beliefs, gain a great support system that will feed you with positive ideals and make you feel good about yourself. Build upon your inner strength and know that you are a strong wonderful and great person who exudes goodness and learn to believe in yourself in anything you do. Know that you can succeed at anything and accomplish anything you want to in your life. Focus on being positive in anything you do and take part in for this will increase your levels of strength and confidence within.

Never allow yourself to feel down about yourself or about matters in your world and never allow others' opinions of you or anything you do bring you down.

Rid our lives of toxic people and those who aren't there for our benefit

Toxic people in our lives are of no benefit to us and it's imperative that we rid our lives of these menacing people for they do no good to us and do anything they can to thwart us in our lives and within our goals and ruin what they can for us.

Toxic people have become a huge problem for people in life. They are full of negative ideations and will do anything to hurt or hamper us in life in various ways. Many people tend to allow toxic people and negative people into their life and will generally tolerate the abuse or negativity that these people show towards them. Some people become accustomed to this abuse even though they don't welcome or warrant it and will ignore it because they feel they need that person in their life or because they feel they have no other choice and can't stop that person. It's important to rid your life of these types of toxic people, and have extremely minimal contact with them and make sure that you don't allow them into your world and that you don't allow their opinions and behaviors to affect you or be a part of your life, life in shape or form.

The most important thing is to have minimal contact with toxic people or no contact into eliminate them from your life completely because they do nothing except create extreme amounts of negativity, anger and hatred, affect your entire life and future through their Nate, very natures in the behaviors that they do towards you.

Have a positive perspective and seeing the 'bright side of things'

The world we exist in is full of uphill battles, and although it's a beautiful and positive place to be in, it can be riddled with negativity, traumas, awful experiences, and scenarios that are not beneficial or good for a person to have undergone. It's a good idea to perceive ideas in life through the lens of love and positivity and to have a positive healthy perspective of events and situations that have occurred in a person's life, everyday life, and every aspect in which they exist in.

Have a positive perspective towards negative things in life

Having a positive perspective towards traumatic or difficult experiences that have occurred in a person's life and leaning or harvesting that perspective to fit your ideals in order to be able to cope with the given situation and to allow your perspective to not allow these kinds of experiences to destroy you completely or ruin your life, mind or being completely.

Having a positive perspective towards negative aspects in life is something that should be done on a daily and even a momentary basis. You should always harbor positive and good perceptions towards anything in your life that happens to you for nothing that usually happens is harrowing or life-threatening and even if it is, it can be a situation that is something that you can deal with or are able to handle. So how can you have a positive perspective towards anything negative that happens in your life? It's through a series or methods of practicing mindfulness, living in the moment, generating positive energy within yourself, being a calm, rational person at all times, and utilizing various positive energies around and within yourself in order to create a harmonious event of nothing but positive energies within yourself and in your being at all the times. Practicing mindfulness is just a form of practice that involves being aware of the present moment without judgment or interpretation. It's often used as a therapeutic tool to help manage stress and improve other conditions. Mindfulness can be practiced through meditation, yoga, or other techniques, or just living in the present moment and enjoying every experience and moment in your life through the means of happiness, positivity, love and goodness. Be aware of your surroundings, and of yourself. You will also need to accept what happens in life without any form of judgment. Be present within your life, and be engaged in what is happening, be kind to yourself and to others as well. Living in the moment is an important technique to use to just harbor happiness and enjoy each and every moment in your life and world, rather than ignoring the moments in your life or not recognizing their importance or creating positive energy for them. It is about recognizing every moment in your life and living in those moments with fulfillment, enjoyment, and extreme positivity.

Utilizing various positive energies within and around yourself can be done easily by constantly thinking positive thoughts and being in a constant state of positivity. Once you've practiced this regularly, you're able to create positive energies in different forms and allow these energies to take over your life and let them be a part of your soul and very being and they tend to seep into your life and your experiences and world and create more harmony and peace.

Your perspective in the situation matters too- you will need to have a very neutral perspective towards aspects that happen to you in your life. Sure, things happen and people can get angry or frustrated over big things in life, and even the smallest of mishaps, but you'll need to have a very subjective perspective and view on the matter and focus on being internally positive, calm and happy despite all the negative things that may be happening around you. This is how you can reach forms of mindfulness and remaining calm in the matter and during any given situation.

Enjoy your experiences in life and be grateful for the people in your life

It's important to enjoy your experiences in life and always be grateful for the people in your life. Often, people tend to take for granted the people that are present in their life and will usually perceive them as lesser, inferior or not as important in their world, when the opposite reality is true- these people are the most important people in someone's world and should be perceived as such. It's a good idea to be in a state of praise and desire for those people in your life, your friends or family rather than taking them for granted for this helps build on positivity and happiness in your world and positive beliefs and ideals.

Enjoy every experience you have in your life and world and love each and every moment and be appreciative of all the great things that life has to offer. Life is an abundant and beautiful blessing that we all should love, cherish and never take for granted, and needs to be experienced and cherished all the time. Rather than not caring about the little experiences you have in your daily world, you should enjoy these situations and scenarios and never ignore them but perceive them as small blessings and this, too will build on positivity and positive states in your life and world.

Learn to recognize your own feelings, beliefs and intentions

Our intentions are extremely important, for living a life with good intent for each and every person, place or thing will generate good intent and will back towards us and will increase good and positive energy in our lives and create more inner bliss.

What we intend for ourselves, and others holds a huge importance in a person's daily world and life. Intending bad for someone usually carries negative karma and negative outcomes, whereas wanting good for someone comes with good karma and great outcomes in life. We need to learn to understand our own feelings, beliefs and intentions and do this through meditative and other practices and this will allow us to become people of a greater and higher awareness and will allow us to harness more goodness in our life and build on good energies, harmonious thoughts and feelings.

A healthy perspective

Your perspective on matters and things in life is what makes the difference between maintaining a healthy state of mind or harboring one which holds negative thoughts or ideas and perceptions. You should always live your life with a healthy and bountiful, beneficial perspective on elements and situations that have occurred in your world, rather than one of a negative nature.

Changing your perspective from a negative one to a positive one can greatly affect the way you perceive outcomes and situations in life and can help you handle and deal with everyday situations, scenarios and allow positivity and love to flourish in your life, rather than negativity or unhealthy perspectives.

If something bad happens in your life, it's important to perceive it with a positive perspective, for then it helps ease the sorrow and negativity associated with the experience, allows you to reframe the situation and look back at it with a positive light which allows for healing of the situation rather than perpetuating negativity which many people tend to do often.

Chapter 3

THE UNHINGED SOUL

The unhinged soul is a greater part of that which is the bright being of our inner selves and realities. We exist in a state of harmony and goodness and need to remember that it's important to live in a place of peace and gratitude, rather than lower ideals or any negative concepts. The soul is the collectively unscathed pure part of our beings which holds the keys and secrets to our lives and worlds we reside in and harbors the pureness and greatness that we are unaware of within our own selves.

The unhinged soul is the part of us that resides within the confines and places of peace and love and a place within that exists in harmony and joy. The soul is such a beautiful, wonderful creation of nature and of God, and allows us to express our innermost feelings through its very nature.

The soul is of a varying nature. It is inherently pure and positive but depending on a person's actions can possess levels of evil and darkness. Our journey to happiness is incumbent on our soul and making sure it is of a positive and pure nature and working on revitalizing it and rebuilding it and making the right choices and actions to ensure we live in a completely positive and harmonious beautiful state of mind in order to allow our soul to become healed, whole and a total state of positivity and purity.

Our internal belief structure

Our internal belief structure guides the pathway for our every being, core and our life. It allows us to be the person we were meant to be and lets us hold specific perspectives about various aspects in life and about the world. We need to harbor a very positive internal belief structure, while staying true to our ideals and the aspects that we were born and grew up with, the beliefs and values that we were once taught, and allow all of areas to guide us as people and make up that which is our internal belief structure. Anything that is of a negative nature, we need to let go of, for in order to truly be happy, our internal beliefs and structure must be engulfed and filled only with positive ideations, thoughts, and concepts.

Our perspective in this life and world are of great importance, and we must live our life with great confidence and a beautiful, wonderful perspective that is of a positive and joyous nature full of goodness, love and life and eliminated from any negative notions of joy, tragedy, negativity, hopelessness and anything of a dark nature. We must exist in a world and internal world and self that exists only in purity, love and light and our souled being generally possesses only this form of love and goodness deep within itself.

Our soul's place

Our soul holds a very special place in our life and world. It is the core of our existence and the place and being where we function and exist without the nature of the physical body. It holds memories of other lifetimes and worlds and is of a completely pure nature and state though it too can be corrupted and hold notions of negativity if a person has accrued negative karma in their life and their soul is of a negative nature. We want our souls to be pure in nature, and in order to do this we must resort to doing only good deeds and focusing on loving goodness, harmony, nature and being only good. This way we can actually cleanse our souls in some form and work on the path to total good and the eradication of negativity and evil in our internal nature and world.

Our soul exists within our physical body, yet it encompasses our physical body and core, and though it harbors an enormous amount of light it too can be comprised of different aspects depending on the kind of person we are. In order to truly be happy, blissful people we will need to work on perfecting our soul and our inner selves in order to become more harmonious, beautiful and better people in general.

The harmony of purity

The beauty of being a pure person full of love and goodness is a major factor and part in being a happy and fulfilled person. It's a good idea to love and enjoy the concept of purity and the essence of innocence and goodness. Many people don't really understand the concept of being in a state of purity or oneness, or of having feelings or thoughts about being a pure and decent human being and person. There are many different paths to happiness and being an internally happy and fulfilled positive, beautiful person inside your soul and being. The many paths to being happy inside your very core can be used to generate great and large amounts of positive and good energy and one way of doing this is by being a pure and harmonious person internally. It's not easy to comprehend this concept for people are generally unaware of this notion and don't understand what it all means. Being a pure and true person allows a person to cleanse their internal self, soul and being in different ways and by different methods allowing a person to feel internal purity, bliss energy and true energetic happiness and fulfillment. The harmony of purity allows us to become whole and pure within ourselves and cleanse our internal selves and be pure like our souls and higher selves. It is one of the blessed gateways to internal bliss and true happiness and is one of the few means and methods to feeling beautiful and pure bliss energy within our soul bodies.

A soul's spiritual nature

The soul possesses a nature of beauty, love and light. It is untouched, untethered, beautiful and full of purity and positivity. The soul is the part of the spirit and being that remains amazing and pure and true to itself. It is a spiritual light entity all to itself and is the building block and foundation that allows goodness and bliss energy to seep into our every being, core, energy and physical body. We need to learn to tap into the oneness of the soul and from then on, we will be able to obtain pure light energy, bliss and let it encompass our very being. The soul actually possesses pure light energy, so this is one important way of accessing an important part of happiness, bliss and joy energies and that is to tap into and access the part of our every core and soul.

The nature of the spirited being

The soul is the part of the spirit that speaks to us in our everyday life and world. It exists within our nature and guides us in our everyday lives whether we believe or know about it or not. The soul is the greater part of our whole being and is the portion of us that lives on and exists whether our body is present. It is greater than our human body and is unscathed and exists within its own nature. Happiness can be attained by knowing and having a greater connection with our own soul and its purpose. The soul has the capability of reaching higher states of bliss and attaining extreme levels of happiness and allowing our human selves to experience these varying forms of happiness and jubilation within.

We exist in varying states of happiness, goodness, negativity, evil and harmony. Every human soul possesses its own place of where it resides in and is available to assist the human body in reaching heightened states of goodness and happiness. It is a beautiful amazing, spirited creation of God that exists in its own space.

Our soul exists for good reason and to help build the channels of positivity and good within our bodies and spirits. Our soul is the gateway to the treasured secrets of our lives and realities and holds mysteries we have no knowledge of. It is a beautiful special spiritual aspect of our world and life.

Hope in our everyday lives

hope is a great part of our soul and life and allows ourselves to build the path to love in other areas of our world. Hope is the key to allowing us as humans to create a brighter future for ourselves and to pave the way for greater treasures along the line to a better life. Hope is a blissful. It's important to live in a world where you're focusing on the good aspects of your world and life and blessed with ideations of hope and a positive world for yourself and your reality. We are hopeful in anything that we do or that we live in and build upon. Hope is what allows us to gain a desire or allows us to need or gives us a yearning or want for something in our lives that we are in a need of.

As humans we are in great need of something higher than ourselves that we can look to for a need or for expectations. Love and happiness are incumbent upon specific expectations and

What is hope in our world. Hope is what we so desire in our lives and what allows us to plan and need and builds the gateway to being a great person and allows someone to be the person they were meant to be.

Grace and Courage in our world

Grace is the beauty we all strive towards and the peace we hope for all of our lives. It allows us to cherish the moments we reside in and flow through the bridges of harmony in vast areas. Grace allows us to be grateful for the little things we possess in life, and for all the things that exist within our worlds. We exist in harmony within our worlds for the sake of being a part of ourselves and we live in a place of peace and love. Grace allows us to appreciate the little things we hold and cherish near and dear to us and lets us be the happiest of people that we can be.

Courage is a great indicator and experience we fall forth into in order to allow us a greater desire to harness our inner strengths and allow the pursuit of greater tasks and lets us push forth towards greater strength and prosperity in our world

Courage allows us to step up into the principles we hold within ourselves and our inner beliefs and desires and lets us express those inner notions and values into various aspects of our everyday lives. We possess great strength within our being and souls and need to delve deep within in order to grab the beautiful ideations within and further develop our inner strength.

Courage is a great indicator and experience we fall forth into in order to allow us a greater desire to harness our inner strengths and allow the pursuit of greater tasks and lets us push forth towards greater strength and prosperity in our world

Courage allows us to step up into the principles we hold within ourselves and our inner beliefs and desires and lets us express those inner notions and values into various aspects of our everyday lives. We possess great strength within our being and souls and need to delve deep within in order to grab the beautiful ideations within and further develop our inner strength

Love light peace and harmony can bring forth blessings into our world and realities and consume the good we hold creating amazing transformations into greater desires and manifestations of strength and virtue.

Chapter 4

Happiness In Our Everyday Lives

Happiness in our everyday lives

Our everyday lives can be full of all kinds of circumstances and situations that we aren't sure how to deal with or resolve. We live in a world where people are in a rush to do things, there are situations which we aren't able to deal with and there is negativity in what we tend to do. We yearn to be happy in our life and seek out experiences that we find beneficial or that can assist us with becoming better people and that fulfill our needs.

Spend time with loved ones

It's important to spend time with loved ones, those who care about you, friends and family and have a very strong and healthy support system. Having an amazing support system can allow us to be incredibly happy people internally and builds up our confidence and self-esteem levels. We need to appreciate and cherish those close to us rather than take for granted those who are near or dear to us which tends to happen sometimes.

Relax and focus on the positives

Relax! For it's a good idea to live your life in comfort and happiness, rather than being in a state of worrying and in a state of hustle and bustle. Are you constantly in a busy state of mind or always wanting to rush somehow? That's not always the best state to be in. Life is very short, so you'll want to relax and focus on the positive aspects of your life and never allow the negatives to affect you in any way, shape or form. Be happy with the things you possess, the material and non-material things that are in your possession and simply be happy!

Trust your instincts

Trust your instincts and the concepts that you believe in and agree with. It's important to focus on the ideas that you feel are right and that you believe or trust in and to focus on the concepts of good and really hone in on these aspects. Believing in your instincts allows you to gain a greater sense of confidence and lets you believe in the various aspects of yourself that you ordinarily wouldn't have the concept of understanding or even acknowledging.

Build upon compassion and grace

Building upon compassion and grace lets us focus on those areas of love, joy, peace and compassion within ourselves and lets us engage in these concepts and ideations. We need to incorporate the concept of compassion in our life, along with grace in order to gain the beauty and love we so desire in our lives. Grace allows us to let harmony flow through our soul and the wonderful concepts of goodness and peace to lift up our spirits and elevate ourselves within a world of love and harmony.

Living in a world of peace and bliss

Living in a world of peace and bliss is an important and special part of existing and being on this planet. We all strive to live in peace and harmony, and most people yearn to live in peace, but their current realities don't always allow for that. If you want to live in a state of peace, you have to learn to overcome obstacles and negativities in your life and within your mind in order to achieve this feat.

People don't necessarily yearn to live in a state of peace or focus on trying to exist in states of bliss. They are generally too busy with their lives and in their own worlds, but we should strive to live in these states of happiness, for then we will always have an internal happiness despite anything that happens in our life, and it aids us during times of grief, stress, or negativity.

Overcoming negativity

Overcoming negativity is a very key step when it comes to being a happy and fulfilled person and for building various states of happiness within a person's soul. Negativity has a horrible impact on all of us. People often tend to live in very negative states however, it's imperative that we focus on undoing This type of darkness and these types of thoughts. Negativity tends to have a very dark injury impact on our lives, and it's important to rid ourselves of this. Any way shape we can.

Focusing on beneficial ideas and aspects in our life is detrimental to eliminating negative ideals and beliefs and allowing the true form of happiness to take place in our world and shape our reality. This isn't always an easy thing to do. There are many ways to deal with negativity and many if them include being spiritual, being positive and love and light, repeating affirmations, focusing on our blessings and loving every moment we live in and cherishing it. These are just some of the few key methods to rid yourself of negative ideations, and to overcome any form of darkness and anger that is present within you.

Never take your blessings for granted

Your blessings are a very important part of your life. Everything that you own and that is a part of your life is something that you should be grateful for in a huge way and appreciate all of the time. You need to focus on appreciating all of your beautiful, wonderful things that you own or possess and not take them for granted as many people tend to do.

Many people most of the time take for granted, the many blessings that they do possess in their life. They don't focus on being appreciative of the little things in their world and are constantly complaining or not focusing their attention on loving and appreciating these aspects in their life. It is imperative to be extremely grateful for the little blessings in your life and the big things as well. Do you often contemplate on what you do possess and how it affects your life whether it's negative or positive?

If you don't, it's a good idea to try to focus on this and wonder how you can better your way of thinking and learn to live in the moment and love everything that you do have in your life and world, and be extremely grateful for it rather than be pessimistic about it.

Being true to your own self and nature

It's always a great idea to be true to your own self and to nature and to stay true to your beliefs and ideals. This is a huge positive step in staying a happy person and always focusing on the good in things and being positive rather than negative.

Strategies on how to deal with negative situations in your everyday life.

Don't let the situation hamper your mood

We often allow situations in our life to hamper our mood and bring us down and let it affect our day in general or the rest of our day. It's good to remain calm and not let life's worries and problems upset us or ruin our mood. This is an easy thing for anyone to do with some practice and self-awareness as well. Remember that life is full of all types of scenarios issues and problems and these problems should not affect you in a negative way and you should have the armor to be able to handle or deal with these problems in an effective and strategic intelligent manner.

Focus on the positive things happening in your day

One important strategy to learn is to always remain in a state of positivity and joy so that the negatives don't affect you as much. Learning to encapsulate your very soul and being and engulf it in a total state of goodness bliss and good energies is what your major focus is going to be on.

If you are in a constant state of happiness and harmony within your heart and mind then the negatives don't really affect or bother you and they become more of whispers in the background rather than major things that bring your mind and soul down or make you angry or upset.

Generate a constant state of positive energy

Generating positive energy is something you need to learn how to do and with practice you can fully understand how to create different types of energy within yourself, being and very body and it is an amazing feat and achievement for with this positive energy you create utilize and harbor will you be able to remain in a constant state of happiness and true calm and peace and be able to tackle an objective or obstacle with a radiating sense of calm and lack of anger or any other low emotions that might be present.

Never get angry about anything

Anger will always breed anger in any form and it is imperative that you remain calm within and always harbor a calm and soothing demeanor inside your soul. The way to do this is to practice possessing this internal calmness and happiness and letting negativity and bad situations bounce off you within your chest area and your heart chakras.

Remain calm cool and collected internally and practice this regularly.

Maintain a sense of peace internally

You need to maintain a constant sense of peace within your mind and inside of your very core and soul. It's not always easy to harbor this form of peace and it's a situation that takes practice through meditations breathing exercises and constant maintenance of harmony and good energies within your very body and self. When you breathe- practice exhaling any negative energies thoughts or feelings and inhaling goodness love and light. You will then need to inhale and exhale all of these energies together and will be creating numerous forms and variations of positive energies.

Once these energies become a regular part of your soul and energetic body, they will automatically flow through you and be able to heal your body and even be able to heal others. They will allow you to maintain an amazing sense of calm and peace within and will become your very core and being and any negative situations or bad feelings will no longer exist within you. These energies allow the beauty of love, light, peace and joy through numerous vibrations flow through your very core on a steady and regular basis.

How to increase happiness in your life

There are many ways to increase the levels of happiness in your life. Your happiness and world matter more than anything and you will want to do what you can to grow and become a happier and better person in general. Here are just some methods and ways you can increase happiness levels in your life.

Eliminate toxic and negative behaviors from your life

Have a positive support system

Having a positive support system is a fundamental way of being able to allow a person to assist themselves with being able to handle and deal with life's situations and with dealing with issues that are occurring in a person's reality. It's important to have a large number of positive influences in one's life in order to be able to function in a healthy aspect within life and society.

A positive support system is a necessity in order to increase happiness levels in a person's life and to help and aid or support a person's life, mental health and personal growth.

Break free from the monotony of your life by adding new experiences

Many people tend to live in a world full of monotony and may be tired of dealing with their current lives. It's important to live in a world where you're encountering various experiences and changing the different scenarios in your everyday world. People live in states of monotony and repetitiveness a lot of the time and need to experience different things in their life in order to build on their future and create a new foundation and new reality for themselves.

Focus on the good aspects in your life

It's important to focus on all the good and healthy pieces and parts of your life and your world and reality. Your world is important, and you need to focus on your interests and goals and all the good things that are occurring in your life. Is there something good happening in your life such as family, friends, a job, or maybe a hobby that you are partaking in? Once you place your focus and attention on the good and positives in your life, you can begin to witness the increase of positive and good things in your world.

Be grateful for the blessings in your life

Be grateful for all the little blessings in your world and cherish the little things that happen in your life and reality. It's important that you're constantly focusing on all the good things rather than the negative.

Exist within a paradigm of seeking to improve in life

It's a great idea to want to improve your life and not remain stagnant and be stuck in the same state of mind, the same job, lifestyle or habit that you've had for a long time. Most of the time people, fear, or don't care for change in their life. Some do but for many they remain stuck and trapped in their present and current jobs, and they are often either unhappy, depressed, or unaware of their current place in their reality and their current state. They don't focus on the concept of improving their life or have the yearning to want to improve their life, change things or even have other goals in the world.

People need to change their perspective in a situation like this, and truly focus on improving their life and their lifestyle and setting goals to improve their world rather than remaining stagnant and doing the same thing that they have been doing for a very long time for this will change their life in a hugely positive way, and allow them to become stronger and better people, and grow and experience the concept of growth.

This also allows them to experience and have new experiences in life, and grow in other areas as well rather than stay in the same situation that they are in. It's a very good idea to understand the concept of growth and improvement and its importance in someone's life and to harness this opportunity and utilize it to the best of your means. By having goals, seeking to improve your life and achieving these goals slowly you'll experience a newfound growth in your world, and it will allow you to then grow further and have amazing and unlimited opportunities as a result.

Chapter 5

How To Escape The World of Negativity

Negativity is a part of our everyday lives. People in this world tend to exist in a whirlwind of all kinds of emotions and feelings and being negative seems to breed within the existence of the planet. Being negative is not a normal phenomenon of how a person should ever feel. People were meant to be happy and positive and live a good existence within their reality, past, present and current. Our society is riddled with negative ideations, concepts, emotions and feelings. Turning on the news all a person can find is a host of negative events, beliefs, ideas and even tv shows are full of morbid and gory concepts rather than positive, decent emotion charged, family-oriented ideals and teachings. There are horror movies, shows, and detective police dramas everywhere on television, rather than heart-felt beautiful family shows that used to exist somewhat in the past at least. It's easy to get caught up in the whirlwind of chaos and negativity that has become of society and cater to its teachings rather than upkeep a positive and harmonious state of mind which is something that a person can become ingrained with.

People have become accustomed to that which is abnormal, out of the ordinary, dark, gloomy or bad for a person's soul. They however don't realize that they've become numb to this darkness rather than finding it abhorrent or something that is difficult to handle or witness because they are not in touch with their own emotions and ideations, haven't sat down to contemplate their reactions or feelings towards these phenomena, and simply don't ponder upon these ideas in their life or world. These negative ideations have become intertwined within a person's soul, mind, psyche, positivity and has created a yin yang effect within their very essence. People simply harbor dark feelings, beliefs, or ideations within themselves and aren't able to effectively eliminate these things within themselves and really don't care to either.

Recognize how you feel within yourself and any dark or negative thoughts or feelings you harbor

If you want to master your emotions and rid yourself of any negative thoughts or beliefs, you will need to examine your emotions internally and attempt to figure out how you feel about different aspects of these emotions in general. Have you ever tried to examine thoughts or feelings you've had internally or any pessimistic or depressive feelings you've had? Have you had recurring bad thoughts about an idea or concept?

You will want to thoroughly and carefully examine any negative thoughtform or feeling you have and try to understand exactly where it comes from.

Are you down on yourself? Do you dislike a certain kind of tv show or person? try to understand where this thought comes from, and not only replace it with a positive one, but very carefully go to the root source of this thought and attempt to eliminate it altogether. Are your thoughts confused or restricted? Do you harbor negative thoughts sometimes but want things to stay and be far more joyous and beneficial for you?

In order to fully eliminate these thoughts, you will want and need to focus on where they're coming from and the source of the negativity. You will then want to further examine and understand what is going on with the thought and from there decide to go ahead and eliminate it altogether by replacing it with a positive one to dissolve the thought or feeling, and by having positive thoughts internally rather than negative ones.

How do you react to negative or dark stimuli you perceive

Negative or dark stimuli is everywhere in our world. When we turn on the tv, read the news or the internet it is simply just there. We live in a society where there are scare tactics being used to confuse and manipulate the masses overall.

How do you react to this dark or negative stimuli that you are exposed to the majority of the time? Do you embrace it? Not let it affect your general mood? Have you become accustomed to it or even numb to it? It's important to understand how we feel towards these negative ideations taught in our society that are everywhere because we need to fully understand our feelings towards these aspects and how it has affected us. This allows us to determine what kind of people we are internally and what kind of perspective we hold about ourselves, our lives and where we are at in our own world.

For instance, if we have become numb to this negative method of thinking and living, we may be in a state of trouble for we may be in a constant state of negativity ourselves and have become used to this or find it normal. Our subconscious minds have become accustomed to this and are used to thinking and living this way when in reality we should feel disturbed by this material and should be geared more towards a very positive state of mind and feeling disturbed by it.

Those who feel disturbed and at a lack of ease from these negative beliefs, and ideals being presented to them, should be living in a state of awareness and recognizing their own thoughts and emotions and should be at a lack of ease and disturbed by this very information rather than numb to it and not caring. We often become what we take in, perceive and watch and it is important to feed ourselves positive concepts and ideals rather than negative ones that we find on the TV or in other places in society. Recognizing your thoughts emotions and being in a higher state of awareness will allow you to become a happier person overall and not fall into the trap of being affected by all the pessimistic and dark news there is in our society.

Also negative feedback can do more damage to a person and even hurt them by causing more issues with past traumas they have dealt with in life and will create more havoc for them in general.

Eliminate the concept of any negativity within yourself by willing it away

One way of eliminating the concept of negativity in your life is by willing it away. You will simply want to think of the source of the negativity and what is causing this feeling to occur within you, and you will want to slowly focus on what this is. You can easily will it away by pushing it out of your mind, your mind's eyes, or your aura and reducing any feelings you have been associating with it.

This is a concept that takes practice and is not easily done. By focusing on the thought and pushing it away from your internal vision and mental state you can completely remove it from your point of view and from yourself.

You can also replace the negative thought or concept by replacing it with any positive thoughts and this is another method you can use to remove it from your state of mind or from yourself. Replacing the negative thought with a positive one is a way of reframing the thought or situation and perceiving it with a more positive light or eliminating it from existence within yourself completely.

Separate any negative feelings or beliefs you have within yourself or about yourself from any positive ones you have

You will want to separate any negative feelings or beliefs you have within yourself from any positive ones. You can do this internally by thinking of all the negative feelings and thoughts you do have within yourself, and all the positive ones and writing them down on paper. By writing them down on paper, you will begin to access them through words and this in turn will allow you to begin to make them tangible sources that you can easily access or even think about and begin to work on. This is one of the few effective ways of being able to eliminate the negative thoughts and sources you have within yourself, and turn them into positive, beneficial ones or eliminate them altogether from within yourself.

The goal will be to remove them altogether and replace them with positive thoughts and ideas. This is an exercise you can work on daily. As you access more thoughts, ideas, feelings or fears that may make you feel negative or down or that are not positive in nature, you can easily begin and learn to remove them from your state of mind and from your very being. The more you practice doing this, the easier it becomes. Your goal will be to have a completely positive state of mind, devoid of any negative thoughts, feelings or irrational fears that many people tend to have very often.

As you eliminate these dark ideas from your very being, you will want to erase them from the paper they're on or cross them out completely. You also don't want to remind yourself of these feelings or ideas because once you're in a completely positive state of mind, you will have forgotten these negative thoughtforms and beliefs.

Eliminating negative self-talk

Negative self-talk exists in a person's life by taking over the beneficial and positive ideals a person may believe about themselves and sets itself in by becoming the dominant voice in a person's mind. Our perception of our life and reality exists in our own minds and what we believe and think about ourselves, and our lives becomes deeply ingrained within the core of our conscious and subconscious beings. Our beliefs shape our reality by perpetuating what we follow, think about, fear, deeply perceive, act upon and what we have become subjected to believing in due to a vast number of experiences and years of suppression and branding within our existences. If we believe we aren't good enough or simply can't follow through or move forward in life or do better, grow or elevate ourselves in a positive manner, we will further create that reality and cause the cycle of negative self-talk to continue to occur. Our very thoughts and beliefs will create this perpetual cycle of usual negativity to continue to occur due to the fact that we harbor these beliefs and feelings in such a strong format, or their very existence will create their presence in our reality.

This negativity and these false ideations and beliefs become so strongly rooted in our minds they begin to create the reality we believe in deep within. What we fear becomes such a strong notion within our mind and spirit that these fears will subconsciously create these fears to occur in our life and world simply by them existing in our minds and our beliefs for or against a particular idea or experience will cause those experiences to become a recurring theme in our lives. The cycle of what we believe and what exists in our minds, souls and subconscious being and spirit continues to repeat itself whether negative or positive as those beliefs and ideations generally shape the reality that occurs within and around us.

Our thoughts and feelings guide, shape and control the reality that surrounds us so in order to change that reality, we must learn to train our minds and change the deep-rooted beliefs and feelings we harbor deep within ourselves, whether we recognize them or not. Even the smallest inkling of a belief or feeling can cause that very notion to occur in our reality and it will continue to happen so long as we believe this is what our life has been should, or will be like due to past experiences, circumstances, or even trauma. The energy we harbor within our minds and spirits projects outward into the world, universe and our reality and can bring forth the circumstances and experiences we may or may not want to occur in our lives.

It is important to reshape and restructure our method of thinking and how we feel about our life and reality. We must learn to train our mind and subconscious minds into harboring positive ideas and beliefs about our world and reality in order for those positive and good concepts to take place in our lives. We must exist in a realm of thinking that is for the benefit of our well-being and that doesn't contain any recognizable fears or toxic events or ideations otherwise those scenarios will continue to energetically be brought forth into our realities by their very presence and existence within our reality and thoughts.

Toxic beliefs and patterns

Toxic beliefs and patterns exist within our world and reality usually due to past traumas, negative experiences and recurring patterns that have existed in our lives and are usually brought upon by one or a few negative recurring themes which harbor unresolved emotions, traumas or have interfered with our energy bodies, souls, and have been left unresolved or are still harnessing those negative emotions and stories that those experiences created. They will in turn be spread outward into the universe and into our world and further create those same scenarios and patterns to occur and will often become recurring themes and events in our lives and if they are of a painful or negative nature, will further perpetuate this cycle to continue. Our universe is a network of varying energies that exist not only in this world but in many others surrounding us and are a result of multitudes of networks of scenarios and situations that have been recurring in our realities for a very long period of time. Scenarios and beliefs that we harbor within ourselves especially those of a negative nature that might be a negative or traumatic situation are released back out into the universe and those very experiences are then recreated due to unresolved beliefs, traumas, fears, hatred, anger, confusion, that have existed within a person's energy, soul body, reality and world.

I believe I deserve goodness, happiness and peace in my life only

I don't believe bad things ever happen to me

I have a very positive outlook in life and towards things that happen to me

I will focus only on the positive and beneficial aspects in my life

Chapter 6

Perspective Is The Key To A Healthy State Of Mind

Your perceptions are an extremely important part of your world and reality and can harbor a great influence when it comes to shaping how you see your world, and how you act, feel, think and the things that happen in your life. We as people tend to have varied perceptions about aspects that happen in our everyday life. For instance, if something negative happens in a person's life, they tend to think that they had a very bad experience and will often focus on the damage or negativity that that very experience did to them and how It influenced their life in a very damaging way. This is not the manner that a person should have when dealing with these kinds of challenging situations.

The way a person should focus on perceiving their situation should be with a different perspective, a positive and beneficial one and one that will create a positive future and outlook for the person. Many negative situations can create unhealed and unresolved traumas and memories. These memories and traumas have a negative and harrowing impact on a person's life and future. People carry with them the burdens of these traumas and allow them to have a negative impact on their life, often creating and causing repeating cycles of the same or similar situations and traumas to occur. This is also because what a person thinks, and a person's thoughts tend to create their reality and the thoughts they put out in their own reality can create the same negative cycles and effects in their world and recreate similar themes and situations. It's important to heal these negative experiences in any way possible that a person can because they will often carry on as a burden in a person's life and create the same cycles and events to repeat themselves and reoccur.

A person needs to look back at the negative events in their life with varying and positive perspectives and different ways rather than perceiving a negative experience as a burden that ruined or affected their life in a negative way. The person committing the acts or situation tend to seek to want the negative act to have an effect on a person for life, and for it to affect or ruin their life permanently, and a survivor of something abusive or negative needs to not allow this to happen. All negative experiences, even severely traumatic ones, can help a person grow and learn from the experience in some form, even though it may not seem this way at first. A traumatic experience can have a very horrifying impact on a person and can damage a person's life, heart and self-esteem and their very soul.

Negative events in a person's life can take a huge toll on their current reality and on their future. They often feel as if their experiences have ruined or destroyed them or their life and carry this baggage with them into their future experiences and create repeating cycles that recreate these exact same patterns. It becomes a cyclical event for most people.

Traumatic experiences can be life-changing for a person, but they don't have to be incredibly negative life-changing experiences. They can be perceived in a positive light rather than something that has damaged or destroyed a person's mind or psyche.

How to perceive traumatic events in a positive perspective

It's imperative to perceive traumatic events in a very positive light rather than a negative one, simply because the importance of having a positive perspective can overshadow any negativity that a person feels about a particular experience they've had.

The grave importance of being incredibly positive can assist a person with changing the perspective of a negative experience and turn it into a good one rather than a negative one.

When we experience negative events there is a negative energetic signature that is associated with this event. It creates negative thought patterns, memories and other cognitive patterns that become associated with trauma and as a result the negativity will perpetuate into a cyclical pattern that continues to occur. We need to reframe our way of thinking and associate those negative events with something positive or look back at it as a positive event rather than a negative one and not let it ruin our lives or our future. We also need to allow our thoughts to recycle into positive ones and never to allow negative events to shape our future or current lives. These situations need to be resolved in a major way rather than sitting and being unresolved and carrying with them trauma energy and symptoms of PTSD which is post traumatic stress disorder.

We must perceive the situation in an incredibly positive light, and look back at the situation, as an experience that we survived, and something that we can grow from, and learn from, and teach others who are going through the same experience and heal others as well. This in turn, allows survivors like us to be fully healed from a scenario like this, move on and grow from a past negative experience rather than let it hinder our current or future reality.

Suppose a very negative event experience happened to a person. Most of the time, people are incredibly upset, angry, or depressed about the situation and aren't sure how to deal with the situation. They tend to be angry, feel very resentful, are confused about how to feel, feel hurt or angry, and feel unsure of how to resolve the situation. They feel the situation is unresolved and aren't sure what to do to make everything okay.

Rather than feeling upset or sad about the situation a person needs to have a plan for how they can handle a scenario like this. They need to focus on being incredibly positive and need to perceive the situation from a different perspective rather than the one they currently have. They will need to be very positive, open minded and not let the situation bring them down, upset them or ruin their life for if they do then they will lose out in the long run and let this very thing hamper them in their life and thwart their growth and stop the good things they deserve from happening in life for them.

Traumatic events need to have a perception change and then and only then can they exist in a scenario where they are perceived in a positive manner and not one that isn't beneficial to the person. You can also rewrite the story of the event in a positive light and this way it can be erased from a person's memory altogether, rather than having a harrowing and negative impact on a person.

Use different perceptions to see the situation through

It's imperative to not allow a negative or traumatic scenario or past situation to destroy or ruin a person's life, and to not let it become a situation that hampers a person's reality in any way. One needs to perceive the situation and themselves as being strong survivors, and to comprehend that they cannot allow it to destroy them in any shape or form or ruin their life. The story of the situation needs to be perceived in a more positive light and even rewritten in a person's mind in a more beneficial manner, rather than a person reliving harrowing memories of utter negativity and dread.

A person also needs to understand that they are stronger and better people and will want to learn from the experience and use it to help themselves in future circumstances and even help others deal with similar circumstances. A person can use these situations to become a helper and healer and teacher of others which can assist them in dealing with the situation as well.

Perceive yourself as a strong person who is a survivor

Others go through negative experiences too, not just me

It was traumatic and painful, but I dealt with it and I won't let it affect my future or life

It was something of the past, and it's done with, and I won't let the person who did it ruin or affect my life in any way

Rewrite the story of the situation in a positive light

Know that if you let it affect you in a negative way, you're giving the person who did it power over your life and future, which is what they wanted in the first place

It helped me grow stronger and I learned from the experience

How to heal past negative events

Healing past negative events can still be done in a positive manner in which the negative event can be done with a perspective of seeing the negative event as positive, not allowing it to ruin your current situation, rewriting the story or situation of the event, and allowing it to be seen as positive or a beneficial experience that has helped a person to grow in different way.

Past experiences that a person has had can have a huge influence on how a person lives their current reality, and how they change or shape their future. Many people tend to look at negative experiences or situations in a negative light and allow these situations to affect them very negatively rather than thinking outside of the box or having a different perspective.

Perceiving the situation with a different and positive outlook and focusing on it as helpful in your life, rather than a burden or painful is one way of being able to thwart the negative effects of a past negative situation that has occurred in someone's life. There's are methods a person can completely change their perception of the situation in order to allow the effects and memories to not destroy them in a negative means, but to allow them to be able to heal and grow from these scenarios and become better, enlightened and stronger people and survivors, rather than weak, broken confused individuals who have undergone a negative or traumatic experience.

Perceive the past situation with a completely different outlook

Focus on how it could help you grow

Perceive the situation with a positive outlook

Focus on the given situation as helpful in your life

Do not allow it to ruin your life or your future

Perceive the situation in a non-negative light and rewrite the story

Shape your perceptions to a more positive point of view

Look back at negative or traumatic experiences in a different light

Your life is governed by your own intentions

Your intentions in the world allow and assist for experiences to take place in your life and world. Your intentions are the driving force behind situations and scenarios that tend to occur in your everyday life. If you harbor good intentions, then you'll exist in a reality where good and positive notions will become a part of your existence and come back to you in many different forms. Having other types of intentions and actions will often create disharmony and negative objectives to take place in a person's life. Negativity tends to breed negativity and will always create for negative experiences in life and negative outcomes in a person's reality. Sometimes things in a person's life may seem otherwise- it may seem as if people who harbor negative intentions have good events happen in their life or that the opposite occurs. That only happens as part of a greater situation in order to make it appear this way. Those who have negative intentions are always going to incur the wrath of negative ideations and experiences only because these people live in a world of negative beliefs, ideals, and seek to want bad for others or have the concept of evil within themselves. It's a good idea to always have positive intentions for others and want good for others and behave with good intent in each and every action you partake in. in order to do this, you must have an incredibly positive state of mind and love the concept of wanting to do good for others and simply seek out the manner of being good and wanting to do good actions for yourself and for others.

Your intentions are part of a greater part of your inner self and can navigate the manner in which you think and behave and affect the greater part of your life. Your intentions can create an effect which causes good or bad things to happen in your life based on the intent you harbor for various things in life and how you feel about others or other people. If you harbor good intentions, then good intent and actions will occur in your life, and recurring patterns of good will happen, but if you harbor ill intentions in your life towards others, it creates a negative effect for those ill intentions to become present in your world. Whatever you project in your world and life out to others, will come back onto you in your own life and create negative effects for you internally, inside your soul and within your energy body and being.

Chapter 7

LIVE WITH THE NOTION OF SELFLESSNESS

Selflessness

Selflessness, generosity and kindness are some qualities that a person must possess in order to generate and harbor true happiness within and to increase and create even more positive energy, love and good in a person's life, world and within their own souls and bodies. Selfishness, evil actions, ill will intent and anything that is negative of nature will tend to create increased amounts of nothing but anger, hatred, negativity and all forms of negative beliefs and emotions within a person. Those who are negative and have all forms of hate and ill will towards others or those who abuse or harm others in any form will be riddled with toxic, dark and evil energies, belief systems, dark lower predators feeding off them, and are people who lack any form of true happiness, bliss, self-awareness and are people who will never experience any form of true happiness or inner bliss. Their evil actions and behaviors will breed more evil and hate within themselves and their souls and this cycle will continue until they are further engulfed in their evil, hatred and negativity. Negativity breeds more of it so in order to be a happy and blissful person a person must undergo extreme and major forms of selflessness, good, humbleness, lack of arrogance, vanity and pride and must practice being extremely humble, good, loving, caring kind people in order to experience happiness within themselves, their souls, and create more good and positivity for themselves and for others.

Happiness creates amazing, beautiful benefits within our world and our own reality. It exuberates beauty, love, and allows people to exist within a paradigm of flawless hopeful graciousness and good. The beauty of being able to exist within the realm of exuberance and true pleasure deep within is one of the few glowing graces that being in a loving positive happy state of mind allows a person to feel and experience within their world and life on levels that are amazing and unheard of.

Selflessness is the concept of existing in a world where we serve others and not our own selfish benefits and desires. We must strive to do what we can to serve and benefit the greater whole of humanity and others together, rather than just our own selves or for selfish or other gains.

Happiness is an extremely important part of existing on this planet. It's important to possess a level of happiness within yourself in order to be able to function on a daily basis, and accomplish the things that you need to do in this world.

In order to succeed in life, we must possess an abundance of goodness and happiness within ourselves, and we must cherish these feelings otherwise there might be problems in our world and within our life

Happiness exists within our own minds and souls and is a blessing we must embrace while awaking into our own existences and embarking upon the journey upon this planet that is considered to be life goodness and decency in our everyday experiences.

In order to be the best that we can be we must embrace the joy of our everyday existences and experiences and inundate them with large and grand concepts of positivity good and decent ideas and concepts.

Being grateful for all the blessings we are equipped with is only a partial manner and method by which we can formulate great concepts and admiration for all that is good in our world.

Happiness is related to the booming fruition that can be found within our very core and soul and the manner in which we cradle and nurture that goodness we embrace and live within

The concept of true happiness and inner satisfaction is related to being content with your reality and blissful and grateful for each and every experience you undertake and participate in within this reality and life. Every experience Is a gift and blessing providing you with more and more abundance within your life and world.

Stay true to yourself your gifts talents goals dreams and blessings.

It's important to stay true to yourself your beliefs your ambitions dreams desires and goals in life. Your beliefs and virtues are an extremely important part of your internal makeup and what makes you the successful vibrant and vital human that you are to yourself, your community and to this planet. You must always abide by your inner passions, beliefs and gifts and hold true to your beliefs and not stray from these ideations and focus on staying true to yourself and your nature. Others will try to get you to stray from your souls and desires, but you must focus on doing and being what is in your best interest and that of others close to you as well

Happiness is found within your soul body life and mind. It is an integral part of your everyday make up and should consume your entire being in various forms. You should exist in a state of true and real happiness because it is the true state of mind you desire to exist within and the blessing of abundance and pleasure you deserve to live your life and experiences through and through positive ideations and beliefs.

It is important not only to exist within a true state of happiness and bliss but to transfer that happiness and graciousness onto others as well and to spread goodness and love to those around you and to those in life in order to promote positivity and blessings to others.

True happiness involves the pursuit of love light and the true essence of being in a state of goodness and bliss and living your life with the notion of truth and righteousness.

Dissolving negativity allows a person to eliminate any and all negative ideations, beliefs, and notions in order to flow within a positive and beneficial state of harmony and mind.

Living through the lens of love not fear

We must live through the lens of love and not fear. fear is a very negative ideation that has held its roots in people's lives and most people don't understand how the concept of fear works. People harbor many emotions deep within them from past experiences and from traumas they have incurred throughout their lives. from these experiences, many feelings and situations arise and as a result they are bombarded with the concept of fear, hate, anger, confusion, haste, angst, and many other negative emotions that build up and become a part of their very being and mind. Love is

Never allowing others to dictate your perception of yourself

Many of us tend to doubt ourselves and our own perceptions. We often feel as if we're just not good enough or as if others are above us in some form. People take their own selves for granted and often feel as if they aren't good enough for some people. People allow others to harbor perceptions about themselves and it tends to affect their daily lives and their own thoughts about themselves. It's imperative to not allow others to dictate your own perception of yourself. Never allow someone else's idea of who you are, change who you are, bring you down or affect your own perception of yourself. You are a strong, confident, individual who can grow to become an even better person and this is the most important aspect of your life that you need to know.

Believe in yourself and your thoughts and intentions!

It's a good idea to believe in yourself in every little thing that you do and allow your thoughts and intentions to help you grow as a person. Once you believe in yourself, you can help others and use your abilities to do great and amazing things and help and heal others on a much greater basis. Your thoughts and intentions should be of a good nature, and you should be doing things with the sole benefit of wanting good for others and for yourself too in order to become a happier and more fulfilled person.

Giving to others, being of charitable help, doing good deeds

Living your life to aid the foundation of others and to focus on being at peace and helping and volunteering your time and abilities to assist others on this planet is one important way of allowing yourself to harness and gain true happiness and nurturing your soul within in order to allow it to grow and develop. Helping others and being of benefit to others is an important part of being a conscious creation on this planet. Many people don't think of the concept of helping and doing to others good as far as being a method to elevating a person's happiness, though it is an important aspect of being in existence in this reality. Giving to others goodness and positivity further creates a snowball effect of allowing that good to return right back to the sender and can create a deep sense of purpose and fulfillment within a person's being. One of the fundamental purposes of existing on this planet is the very concept of having the great opportunity to aid and be of assistance to others and to be able to give your time and efforts into spreading joy, good and love to others. It is a true gift, blessing and means that should bring an abundance of happiness and joy to others to be able to undergo and fulfill.

The belief in truth love and harmony allow us to become better people and exist within our worlds in a greater state of true happiness and greater calm. The aspect of spreading love and good allows us to let that peace grow within our souls and energies.

Living through the lens of peace and bliss allow you to perceive life with the notion of joy and create a greater sense of fulfillment and happiness

Your beliefs and ideations shape who you are within your soul and being and allow your mind to become honed into these perceptions and ideations

Finding peace within you means allowing varying aspects of love and good to flow within your being and become introduced into your life

True peace can exist in a myriad of formats but can safely be found and experienced within the scenario of a sound and sane happy healthy mind that is connected to the soul and universe through a mutual energy that is in a constant state of harboring and channeling positive good energies in hundreds of forms and by creating more positive energy through beliefs actions experiences good deeds and by giving and sending out mass forms of positive and good energy and vibes. Bursts of peace bring forth various forms of happiness and jubilation in a person's life and world.

Ideations of attaining enlightenment can attribute to experiencing various forms of happiness and love within a person's world and inner self and can lead to many experiences of bliss and ecstasy and jubilation and the desire to gain and attract more and spread more to others which in turn will bring it back to the sender unknowingly.

Morality is the gateway to inner bliss

In order to truly be happy a person must exist in a world where morals are the forefront of their world and must live and abide by an inner moral code and decency. True morality and living within the confines of seeking to be moral deep within and being a truly moral person with righteousness, goodness and values can create a world of happiness within and is one of the keys to experiencing true happiness and joy within a person's soul and life. If a person is blessed with goodness and morals within their being and aura, and seeks to live by these ideals and feelings, they will experience many forms of true bliss within themselves and in their life, for the emblem of happiness is seeking and doing good and obtaining truth, justice, goodness and true morality within a person's self.

Being a moral person allows a person to become happier and more enlightened and in a state of bliss and goodness. It's important to do good deeds and focus on doing good in everything that you do and with every intention that you harbor. Morals are an important part of a person's everyday life. People often tend to forget about moral standards and codes and live by other standards rather than the morals they are meant or supposed to live by.

We all desire to experience endless bounds of happiness, positivity peace and enlightenment. We choose to experience our lives and realities by the lens we harbor within our internal selves. Living a life through the lens of positivity and joy allow us to expand our inner joy and experience a large amount of happiness peace and pleasure. Happiness and positivity are part of our reality and we seek to express happiness and goodness and exist in a state of harmony and positivity any chance we can get.

Spreading positivity joy love and goodness to others can increase our inner levels of joy and allow happiness to gain growth and spread within our being. The more positivity we give out, the greater we experience ourselves. Increasing joy in our lives can contribute to a greater sense of health, wealth and wellness and allows us to immerse ourselves in a reality of pleasure and happiness rather than one filled with negativity or angst.

Chapter 8

THE BEAUTY OF BEING YOU

You are a wonderful amazing powerful beautiful and special individual. There is a beauty and greatness that comes within each living being that exists on this planet, and there is a good hope that comes with each interaction that occurs with every soul. It's important to appreciate and respect yourself and understand who you are and live each moment in this world through the lens of love, light peace, harmony and joy and focus on achieving a greater harmony with the appreciation of your being and the person you are within. You are a special important creation in this universe. Your opinion and persona matter and everything you speak, do and say has a huge impact in the world and in the collective consciousness of the universe. Your wondrous nature can bring goodness and love and blessings to the world around you, and it's something you may not have an inkling of being aware of.

You are a special amazing creation of God and someone who is important and special. Your thoughts and feelings and world matters and the things you do and partake in are of grave significance. Do you believe in yourself and the things that matter to you and do you believe in the things that you represent and hold near and dear to you? If you do that's a great and wonderful thing. Holding moments that are of significance are important matters in your life and world. You hold the key to doing amazing, great and beautiful special things in your life and in the world of others. It's important to appreciate every little thing about yourself and recognize the small and little things and all of the achievements you hold within your world.

Recognizing your achievements and successes

Recognize your achievements and successes. They are of intricate importance and really enjoy the success you've achieved and who you are. This will help you further appreciate who you are as a person.

People often take for granted their achievements or tend to forget about them. You will want to often remember the things you have achieved so as to appreciate the blessing of yourself and the beauty of yourself, and constantly remind yourself of the good things you deserve in life. Focusing on loving yourself and wanting good for you will in turn make you want good for others as well and build on positivity and good ideals for those around you and allow you to become a beacon of happiness and good for you and everyone in your presence.

The simplicity of being yourself

It's important to focus on the simplicity of being yourself. You are the most important person in your universe aside from those who you love, appreciate and cherish and you will want to be yourself and not try to be someone else or be fake in any form.

Recognizing your self-worth

Appreciate your self-worth. It is the most important part of you, and you will need to acknowledge how important you are and that you matter in this world and your worth is of extreme importance. Don't ignore your self-worth, sell yourself short, or take yourself for granted.

Appreciate the small things about yourself

It's good to appreciate the little things about yourself, the things that you don't tend to focus on or are unaware of. All the wonderful aspects about yourself such as your shortcomings, your faults, gifts, goodness are things you need to acknowledge and allow to be appreciated in many different ways.

Learn to love yourself unconditionally

You will need to love yourself in an unconditional manner. You should be the most important person in your universe and not in a narcissistic way. It's important to serve others and be completely selfless but it is also imperative to love yourself and appreciate yourself in order to make sure that you maintain any form of pleasure for if you don't, you'll end up losing yourself in the background of many mixed emotions, negative ideations, traumas, life issues. Your needs matter and loving yourself and practicing self-care is something that should be done on a regular basis. Many people tend to sacrifice themselves and their needs for others and end up in the background of losing themselves and end up losing their self-esteem or parts of themselves. You should love yourself in a humble, kind and non-arrogant way and understand your needs and desires and highlight them in your life. Believe in your dreams, goals, opinions, intentions, wishes and desires. Appreciate the person that you are, and the sacrifices you've made in your life and all the wonderful things you have done.

Practice self-care in many different forms. Take care of your needs and desires once in a while or very often in order to make sure you are at the forefront in your life, and that your confidence is boosted as much as possible. Practicing self-care and loving yourself and your opinions and beliefs will boost your confidence levels and allow yourself not to waver at the hands of predators, negative people or those trying to bring you down or hamper you or your life.

Eliminating any form of arrogance or negativity

Eliminating any form of arrogance is one path closer to becoming a happier and more fulfilled person. The reason for this is that arrogance and any negative qualities in a person breeds negativity, and those who are negative, or hold any forms of evil or malice within them, are never or will never be happy people internally or in general.

People often think that those who hurt or bully others or those who victimize others are happy people or have better lives. Many people deal with abusive situations in their world and believe or feel as if those who've abused or hurt them have a better life than them. They feel as if their life or world has been stolen by these people and it very well may have been for a period of time, however the person committing the crimes of abuse were never happy or good people to begin with. Those who commit any forms of abuse possess no form of happiness, joy or internal happiness. These are incredibly negative, jaded confused dark people who harbor many issues within them internally.

Sacrifice your needs for others

Sometimes it's good to sacrifice your needs for those of others, though you don't want to get caught up in it too much. When you become selfless and serve others, it helps build internal strength, character, and allows you to become a positive emblem of glory and goodness for yourself and for those around you.

Never fear others or their perceptions of you

People tend to fear other people's perceptions of their own selves or care too much about what other people think. Though it is healthy to care what others think, and to want to make sure there is nothing wrong with you or that you're doing well in general, it's a good idea to focus on your own internal self-confidence and to never allow other people's faulty or negative perceptions of you to affect or influence your self-esteem, personal power or internal confidence. You should never fear others or what they think of you because you should be extremely strong internally and should know exactly who you are and not allow these 'other' external false beliefs to get to you, bring you down or affect your life in any way.

Live in the moment and appreciate the beauty of your life

Live in the current beautiful, special moment and appreciate the wonderful beauties present in your life. Do you have children, pets, family members, friends? Learn to appreciate them and live in the moment and cherish every second you live in rather than ignoring it, living in states of darkness or negativity, or depression. Appreciate these small moments which is what living in the moment is, and appreciate the smaller, important aspects of your life.

Harness your own personal power

Harness your own personal power. Many people do not focus on their own personal power- they tend to forget it exists or don't recognize its very existence. Your personal power is the means by which you hold an extreme amount of power internally to steer yourself in the ways of confidence, harmony, love, peace and a collective power to assist and help you in your life. Learn to recognize where your personal power does exist. Does it exist within you? Have you ever thought about what your personal power truly is? Have you ever tried to access your personal power to attempted to figure out how to access it in order to utilize it for your own personal gain or to help yourself in your own life? If you haven't, this is something you will want to do by focusing on the core of yourself, and what makes you 'you', and what makes you tick as a person.

Learn what your strengths and weaknesses are and determine what your true personal power is, for once you're able to access it, the sky is the limit for you! Once you access your personal power and learn to utilize it and fully understand it, you will be able to do amazing feats and achieve great things. You can also more easily handle aspects in your life and world and can better utilize many other concepts in life in general once you're able to understand where your true power comes from, what it is, who you truly are inside, and how to unleash this part of yourself.

Being you matters in this world

Many people tend to feel as if they are not anyone special, possess no real importance, or don't hold the importance they desire in this world. This is completely untrue, for each and every person in this world is of extreme and utmost importance and possesses a unique ability and place in this world and matters to everyone and to the collective consciousness of the planet. Every breathing, living creation that has a life matters and holds a special place in this world.

Being you matters in this world. Never sell yourself short or think you are not as important as others, for this is completely untrue. Your importance shines through and you matter as a person for your presence has a special importance in this world and you are here to do great things and to assist others whether you know it or not.

The Joys Of Living

Happiness can be expressed in hundreds of ways and by various means in our daily lives. We must learn to experience happiness and perceive positivity and joy through every aspect and experience we encounter and partake in. Every moment in our life, is a glimmer that should be one step closer to generating more droves of positive energy in our world and a method by which we live our momentary existence. When we wake up, we should be grateful and in bliss for all that we possess and all that exists in our life. We should be thankful for the gift of life and being able to exist and experience the joys of living. Life is a blessed gift given to us, so that we can enjoy and partake in every experience and moment and use those moments to spread harmony and positivity towards others and to the collective consciousness of the masses out there. Our jobs are not monotonous sanctuaries whereby we are 'slaves' to a corrupt system designed to deprive us of the goodness of existing in the world. They are places where we can build positive experiences, enjoy the smaller things, learn from everyday experiences and a place where we can generate beneficial relationships, friends and wonderful and new experiences each and every single day. Our perspective within our lives needs to be through the lens of happiness and joy and we need to be free from the bounds and chains of negativity, fear, depression, anger, jealousy, or anything negative or dark and steer clear of this state of mind and way of thinking.

Living a life of prosperity and goodness Is what we strive to do. We need to live in a place of positivity and do good deeds and be a good person to ourselves and to those around us. There are thousands of joys of being alive on this planet and its of grave importance to focus on these great joys and implement them in our everyday lives. Being a joyful and jubilant person in each and every task and experience we undergo allows us to experience these situations in life and lets us build upon that very goodness and move on from there.

Having a positive perspective

Happiness is the bountiful source of love that radiates deep within our spirits and beings and allows us to flourish within the definition of hope and freedom. We exist in a confusing world where selfishness reigns and there are aspects in this world where harmony and peace seem to be non-existent. We want to exist in a reality where goodness is the norm and there is an abundance of pure positive energy and goodness anywhere we journey and within our realities and so we can create this positivity and joy and focus on allowing it to become greater and more widespread

The harmony within our presence can create greater excursions and experiences and allow for a more well-rounded experience in a world of truth and jubilation.

Love, light, peace, and harmony can bring forth blessings into our world and realities and consume the good we hold creating amazing transformations into greater desires and manifestations of strength and virtue.

We are all happy positive people within our core and souls yet that part of us has been taken away in some cases and it needs to be regenerated and brought back in order for us to live a life of total joy and being engulfed in various levels of peace and goodness.

Harmony allows for us to become joyous good people and live the life we so desire rather than be in a state of negativity confusion madness or hurt.

Harmony is the essence and key of our souls and the very part of our spirits that lets us exist in a state of peace and love. Our joy is brought forth through differing means of being happy and good inside our core being. Harmony lets us coexist within our very selves internally and lets our higher self and regular self, meld and become one with each other.

Happiness is a harmonious love you exhibit and find within yourself and your world and it's an important part of your life and bring to feel elated and joyful at all given times within your beautiful wonderful and special life. Your life matters and is of extreme importance and you deserve to feel constant happiness in it not anger, sadness, grief, or any negative emotions or feelings

Ridding yourself of envy. Envy exists in the negative dark realms as a low emotion and feeling that is there to destroy a person's internal makeup pollute the mind and soul and create feelings of inner despair and contributes to forms of trauma and chaos in the world. It is a negative toxic unnecessary thought, feeling and emotion that must be eliminated from a person's state of mind and way of thinking and being. An envious person can never truly encounter any form of true bliss and will always in a state of mental rot and soul pollution.

Chapter 9

Eliminate Traumas and Fears in Your Life

People often go through negative situations in life that can create drastic and dramatic consequences in their world and reality. When a person undergoes a negative encounter or event, they end up facing the concept of trauma and creating this trauma and trauma energy in their body, mind, spirit and world. Going through an incredibly negative circumstance or experience can create extreme amounts of trauma in a person and cause them to feel significant negative emotions such as fear, anger, confusion, angst, depression, sickness, and other types of feelings internally. Trauma can be a significant issue in a person's life and can create a snowballing and spiraling of negative events and effects to occur within a person's life and reality.

What is trauma?

Trauma is an emotional response to an intense event that threatens or causes harm. It is often the result of an overwhelming amount of stress that exceeds one's ability to cope with or accept the emotions involved with that experience.

Trauma can be caused by an event that a person cannot control, or in which there is a perceived lack of control. Trauma victims will often have thoughts of "what if" or "if only" related to the event, in order to gain some form of control of the situation since they had no ability to stop the situation from happening, control its outcomes or circumstances or erase the event from ever occurring.

Trauma may result from a single distressing experience, or from recurring events of being overwhelmed. It can be precipitated over weeks, years, or even decades, as the person struggles to cope with the immediate circumstances, eventually leading to serious, long-term negative consequences.

Trauma creates long-term negative effects in a person and can lead to even more drastic harrowing effects on a person's life and world. A person can end up becoming suicidal, confused, have a host of bleak feelings and emotions within them. Trauma manifests in different forms and can even affect a person's physical body by taking over a person's mental state and seeping through to creating symptoms and issues such as chronic fatigue, fibromyalgia and other medical issues for a victim or person experiencing these recurring feelings or thoughts. Trauma often creates a pattern of recurring thoughts or feelings of an event that occurred or even a perceived event that will lead to unresolved emotions over the outcome of the situation.

Some of the different types of trauma that can occur in a person's life include:

- **Acute trauma** results from a single incident.
- **Chronic trauma** is repeated and prolonged, such as domestic violence or abuse.
- **Complex trauma** is exposure to varied and multiple traumatic events, often of an invasive, interpersonal nature.

When a person is traumatized, many different systems are activated in the brain, the mind and memory are overwhelmed with intense stimulation, and the body's ability to return the mind to its restful state is impacted. The serious effects of trauma can be varied and include many symptoms which can include:

- Memory problems
- Concentration problems
- Psychological distress
- Physiological distress
- Relationship problems
- Social withdrawal
- Fear

- Sadness
- Feeling nervous, jumpy, or on high alert
- Irritability or anger
- Difficulty sleeping
- Intrusive thoughts, flashbacks, or nightmares
- Trouble feeling positive emotions

Often, these symptoms improve over time, though most of the time many people do experience intense, long-term effects that will interfere with their daily lives and may stay for years creating other issues in a person's life. People who experience trauma are at major risk for post-traumatic stress disorder (PTSD), and often develop the disorder and will end up having repeat and recurring patterns or thoughts that take over them and happen a lot that they are unable to control or do anything about. These thoughts and patterns create more fear and intense emotions in a person and as a result they are unable to heal or get over or move on from these past traumatic events and situations. They then take over their life and create more negativity and negative events and it becomes an extreme negative pattern and recurring theme in their life and world.

What is a trigger:

A trigger is a circumstance in a person's life that has can cause recurring memories for a person who has undergone trauma or who carries or harbors any form of trauma in their life. A trigger can be a sensation, taste, sound, experience, object, or anything that can create or cause memories for a person who has undergone negative experiences in their life. It is a psychological stimulus that prompts involuntary recall of a previous traumatic experience. The stimulus itself doesn't necessarily need to be frightening and may be indirectly reminiscent of an earlier traumatic incident, such as a scent or a piece of clothing.

Traumatic situations create increased levels of fear in a person's world and psyche

When a person undergoes a traumatic event or situation, they are left with a host of residue of the situation, intense recurring thoughts and thought patterns of the events which is considered to be post-traumatic stress disorder, and a host of negative and harrowing painful emotions, thoughts, and feelings associated with the past traumatic event that occurred. This creates an intense and great amount of fear within a person and forces them to want to avoid this fear and this past circumstance and situation. Many events and things in their life then become 'triggers' for them so that they do not have to relive or relate to the traumatic event or remember it in any form even if it is repeating in their subconscious and conscious mind through post-traumatic stress and repeat thoughts and patterns mentally.

People will go to great lengths in order to avoid the memory of these traumatic events and feelings or anything associated with it and this can create major issues in a person's life. Some examples of a person having to undergo any form of fear as a result of trauma might be a person withdrawing from society, locking themselves inside their home or avoiding the outside world, minimizing social contact, agoraphobia and avoiding crowds, having forms of social anxiety, being unable to communicate with others effectively, fearing social interactions, and any measure or step they can take to avoid having to relive the painful traumatic situation or have any association with it.

How to deal with and eliminate trauma in a person's life

There are many coping strategies and forms of care that a person can utilize in order to manage trauma in their life. It's not easy to eliminate or deal with trauma and rid yourself of it. Sometimes time does help the situation and the length of time that has occurred will then cause the traumatic event to diminish and become of lesser importance negatively and have a lesser impact on a person, but most of the time a person would need to resort to effective strategies in order to rid themselves of this traumatic memory or event.

Create a positive support system for yourself

Create a support system for yourself with positive, beneficial people and those who are there to help and assist you in your journey and life and can help heal you from the negative circumstances you've undergone. Gather together all the positive and good people you know and create friendships with them and make sure that you're on the wavelength and that they know exactly who you are and what makes you happy, sad, upset, smile and what things matter to you. It's very important to create a solid decent support system for yourself so that others can help you through your healing journey and can help you deal with traumatic events or situations that have happened to you, or things you might be encountering in your daily life currently.

Focus on all the positives in your life

Focus on the positives in your life and all the good things that you do have and learn to ignore the never to focus on the traumatic situations and circumstances. It's extremely important that you do not focus on the traumatic situation as if it Is the most important thing in the world. If a person continues to focus on a negative situation or circumstance, it will consume them and take over their life in repeat negative patterns rather than being eliminated from their world.

You will need to focus on all the good things you do have in your life- your loved ones, friends, family, possessions, pets, children, and everything in your life that is positive, beneficial and that which makes you very happy and that is of a good nature in your world. Do you have friends or family that love or care for you? Do you have children you love and care for who love you unconditionally? Pets? You will need to harbor a lot of positive energy and goodness and appreciate and love all the great positives in your life and the many blessings you do possess and that you have to offer.

Eliminate the traumatic event from your world, life and mind completely

It's important to eliminate this negative situation in your life and rather than perceiving it as the most negative thing to ever happen to you, allow it to become diminished in your world and understand that it holds no importance in your life and world and turns into background noise or music, rather than the most important horrific thing that has happened to you. People tend to give traumatic situations extreme importance in the most negative way possible rather than eliminating them from a person's life and world completely.

Understand that the event that happened to you holds no importance or significance and that you are the only important person in your world and no other person can hurt, harm or bring you down or affect your life. When a person does something negative or bad to you, they are hoping to affect your life in a major way and for the long run. They literally want to destroy your life permanently and make sure that the abuse or wrong they did to you is going to have long-term and harrowing effects on you. You have to make sure that you don't allow this to take place or happen, and that you don't allow the things they did to you or have a long-term effect on your life in any way, shape, or form.

Practice positive affirmations, self-care, harmonizing and energizing yourself

It's extremely important to utilize any form of self-care that you can and taking good care of yourself, having a routine to handle the concept of taking care of you, focus on loving yourself no matter what, and practicing positive affirmations so that you can repeat them to yourself and build your self-esteem and confidence.

Perceive the event with a positive perspective

Perceiving the situation with a positive perspective is the way with which you should be looking at the traumatic or negative situation at hand. You should look at the situation as a very positive one, even if it isn't, rather than a scenario that has ruined or hurt your life in some way. There are various ways a person can do this and one is by allowing the memories to be different, rather than remembering the real experience that did occur. You can also see the situation as positive by understanding that it is something of the past that did happen, and it's not happening anymore, and to understand that you can grow from the situation and become a better person because of it, a stronger person and even help others in similar situations as a result. These situations actually help us become masters and gurus in our lives, and though they are painful and challenging, allow us to become better, wiser and stronger people in the long run as a result.

Allow the situation to let you grow and become a better person

It's important to allow the negative situation to let you grow and become a better person and survivor as a result of it. It's important to perceive yourself as a survivor and someone who has survived harrowing personal situations and events, and someone who is a stronger and better person who can help others as a result of it.

Strengthen yourself your life and your mind

Building on your strengths is of utmost importance. You must build upon your strengths and the wonderful strong nature you have and do your best to be a stronger and better person in general. You are an important person and your life and world matter. Are there things in your life that really matter to you? Do you have aspects in your life that are of importance to you? You will need to build upon your strengths and all the positive things that matter to you in a huge way.

Build your confidence and self-esteem

You must build your confidence and self-esteem in various ways and that your confidence and self-esteem are the things that matter. Your confidence is the most important aspect of your beautiful life, and you deserve to be the most confident and happiest person you can be in your world. If you have low confidence, there can be many problems in your world and life.

You will have a hard time accomplishing many things and you'll have difficulty succeeding in life.

Having a strong confidence comes from deep within your very core. Confidence can help deal with past issues and traumatic issues in life. People who've dealt with trauma have had many issues with their confidence- it has been destroyed in their life. They will need to regain this and can do so by practicing focusing on all the positives in their life and by healing from the trauma they have dealt with. Once you develop your amazing confidence you will be able to better handle any trauma or issues you've dealt with in your life. Build your confidence by constantly reminding yourself of all the great things that are in your life, and anything in your life that is good or beneficial, and even by repeating positive mantras and affirmations to boost your self-esteem.

Focus on being the best person you can be

You will want to focus on being the best person you can be. It's important to be a great and wonderful person and do all the good things you're entitled to doing in this life. Focus on being happy and being positive and being a happy gracious loving soul and person who is living their life to the fullest. Those who've been affected by trauma have had serious issues with development due to the fact that they've faced a lot of negativity in their life and it affects their life and future in a very harrowing way.

You will want to heal from the trauma that has happened so you can be the very best person that you're entitled to being and then you can focus on changing your future from the negative one the trauma and negative ideations have caused you into something very positive and beneficial for you.

Learn to appreciate the life you're living

You will want to learn to appreciate the life you're living and really focus on loving every aspect of the beneficial, fun, great and cool things present in your life. This will help you deal with and eliminate the trauma and bad memories and feelings in your life and world.

Learn to live in the moment

Learn to live in the moment and appreciate every minute and second of your wonderful, beautiful existence. Learn to focus on being happy with every given second of your life. Once you learn to focus and appreciate every minute of your life, it will be far easier for you to handle and deal with any kind of traumatic or negative situation. it will also eliminate any form of fear in your life and help you build on positivity and positive energy in your life.

Love yourself unconditionally

You will need to love yourself unconditionally and love every aspect of yourself and practice good amounts of self-care and focus on the positives in your life. Loving yourself and embracing who you are allows you to become a better person in general and be a better person overall. It will allow you to grow more positive energy and deal with all the negative trauma you have had to experience.

Look at your situation with a positive perspective

Perceive your negative and traumatic situation with a positive perspective. It may be very difficult, but this is one way of being able to overcome the situation. it may have been a negative experience, but you can perceive or see it as a situation that will in fact help you grow and become a better person and allow you to become a stronger and even better person. if you perceive your situation through this lens, then you'll be able to greater accept the challenges you've faced, get over them and not allow them to affect your life.

Use the situation to help others who've been through similar

It's a very good idea to use your negative situation to help others who've been through similar circumstances that you have. Sometimes there are reasons people actually go through these harrowing situations and it's actually to help others as well, who are going through them. Sometimes that's not actually the reason they happen, however you can still use these situations to help yourself become a better person, grow from what has happened to you and use it to learn from your experiences and do what you can to help others in a similar situation. this can also be a very powerful and empowering thing to encounter and deal with once you've started helping others in similar circumstances.

Fear is a grand emotion that traumatic events and circumstances can create or cause

Fear is a distressing emotion aroused by impending danger, evil, pain, etc., whether the threat is real or imagined, or the feeling of being afraid or in danger.

Fear in a traumatic situation is characterized by an emotional state where a person is scared or terrified of a certain feeling, circumstance, situation or emotion and reacts accordingly in order to avoid those feelings or that situation and in order to avoid further negativity, will resort to staying away from a certain situation or will stop from feeling those specific emotions in order to avoid any sort of a breakdown or having to relive a situation.

Fear can become a huge problem in a person's life. People often use fear as a means to mask to avoid specific circumstances especially those who've undergone trauma, and they will go to great lengths to avoid these situations in order to not allow it to trigger the memory of past traumas or situations. Fear in a person's world needs to be eliminated completely, for only then will a person be able to live a healthy life and lifestyle, free of the worries of the past and not allow traumatic situations to haunt their current life and affect their future. Fear often takes over a person uncontrollably who has been through trauma, and they have no real control over this fear due to the fact that they will do anything to avoid any association with the traumatic event and will resort to fearing situations or events in order to avoid any feelings, emotions or thoughts associated with an event that was incredibly negative and painful for them.

Many people in this situation then turn into people who develop various kinds of fears within them and these negative emotions often create snowball effects which in turn will create more negative emotions, thoughts and feelings associated with fear such as angst, depression, paranoia, phobias, and will result in greater negative outcomes for a person. Fear is a huge problem for many people and needs to be eliminated in a person's mind, world and psyche. A person needs to be able to overcome any feelings of fear or any triggers or feelings they do have internally and there are ways and methods they are able to do this.

How to eliminate fear in a person's life

Think positive thoughts only

Think positive thoughts only. If you can master the art of thinking positive thoughts and having no negative ones there, then you're on your way to doing yourself a good service. Constantly think of beneficial good things you can place in your mind such as positive affirmations, goals, happy ideas, and ideal thoughts that a person holds in order to put them in a state of happiness and out of fear.

Eliminate fearful thoughts with positive ones

It's imperative to eliminate fearful thoughts with positive ones. If you're thinking "I don't want to do this" or you're terrified or scared of doing something, then it's essential that you think in terms of "I can do this" or "I can easily do this" or "I will do this."

Face the fear and learn how to eliminate it

You will need to face the fears you've encountered by not fearing them and even allowing the thoughts in your mind to go through and learning how to eliminate these fears and letting them not take over your life and mind. This can be done effectively by being a strong, powerful, confident person who is strong-minded enough to deal with the particular fears you are dealing with. You can also face your fears by exposing yourself to them in different forms in order to allow your mind and psyche to overcome them.

Some ways of facing fears you have to deal with are

Exposure therapy: Gradually expose yourself to the thing you fear, starting with easier situations and working your way up. For example, if you're afraid of animals, you could start by looking at pictures of cats, then standing across the park from a cat just to try to overcome the situation.

Relaxation techniques: Try deep breathing, progressive muscle relaxation, or imagining yourself in a relaxing place.

Mindfulness: Practice being intentionally aware of the present moment.

Find humor: Try to find humor in the situation to make it less intimidating. Attempt to use different methods of humor to try to eliminate the fear completely.

Talk about it: Talking about your fears can help. Try to talk to your situation with close confidantes, family or friends.

Watch others do it: Watching someone else face their fear can help you practice sitting with the discomfort without actually doing it yourself.

Rate your fear: Rate how difficult each situation is to face, from 0 to 100. Start with the easiest situation and work your way up.

Do not allow the fears and triggers to affect you

This is because when a person undergoes a negative or traumatic circumstance, they often perceive the circumstance to be of great or extreme importance, and need many forms of validation, support, justification, help and healing. When they do not receive these forms of healing or care or validation and support, this negative circumstance turns into a majorly traumatic event for them, and it develops into unresolved emotions and traumatic energies within their body and energy body and soul and mind. They then are in dire need of validation, support and healing otherwise the negative event will take over them their lives and their future and world and create more negative events in their life, and a host of negative thoughtforms, emotions and problems.

Prioritize self-care. It's imperative to practice various forms of self-care. Get a good night's rest, work on yourself, journal daily, pamper yourself, and do what you can in your power to take care of yourself and to make sure you're comfortable, relaxed and doing well rather than in a state of fear or stress.

Chapter 10

Gain A Greater Awareness Of Yourself And Others

Gaining awareness of yourself and others is very important in a person's everyday life. People don't fully comprehend the notion of being a higher aware human being. They often live and exist in states of not being aware of their intentions, the way they function and exist, and their very core and self. People often do not get to know themselves or understand what it means to become self-aware or possess a higher awareness in life and in aspects in their world.

Awareness holds many different key characteristics. Awareness allows us to become better people in life, understand how we function and why, and lets us grow into better people overall. Once we become aware of aspects happening in our world, we understand ourselves better and this lets us become better people overall and increases our levels of positive energy and happiness.

What is awareness: awareness is the concept of our knowledge of things great and small and lets us examine our own inner selves, and the reason why we function and tick. There are different forms of awareness we can utilize or partake in.

Higher awareness allows us to become consciously and unconsciously aware of each in our every thought emotion belief, feelings, and perception that we hold and utilize our soul and life. Many people live through the lens of a lack of higher awareness, and they are completely unaware of why they do the things they do and the reason and meaning behind their behaviors and actions and why they function the manner in which they do.

Being a person who exists in higher awareness allows a person to become a more spiritually and aware person that exists in states of higher consciousness and allows a person to get to know themselves and those around them so they can function on a higher and greater level.

Being in a state of higher awareness and awareness in general, lets the general populace and average person exist in a higher state of consciousness and vibration and level of functioning.

Awareness of self

It's of great importance to live your life in this world being a very self-aware person. what is the concept of self-awareness? Self-awareness is the ability to understand and recognize your own thoughts, emotions, and behaviors, and how they impact yourself and others. It's a psychological state where you focus on yourself, as if you were observing another person and fully understand the reasons for your actions, thoughts and behaviors and are fully cognizant of who you are as a person.

Self-awareness is a key component of emotional intelligence and is important for personal and professional growth. It can help you: make better decisions, build healthier relationships, lead with authenticity, take better care of yourself, and live a more fulfilling life. Self-awareness is a skill that develops over time as you learn more about yourself. Once you completely understand your wants, needs, desires and the aspects in life that make you tick, you're on your way to becoming a more fulfilled person. you then can comprehend the different reasons behind your emotions and actions and will know how to react or behave in given circumstances and will become able to witness, monitor and control your actions and thoughts. Adults can help students build self-awareness through activities, strategies, and asking thoughtful questions.

Awareness of soul and spirit

You will need to be fully aware of your soul and spirit. This entails understanding the concept of what a soul is and knowing how to effectively communicate with your soul and other parts of yourself, such as your higher self.

Awareness of our mind and thoughts

We always need to be aware of our present mind and every thought that graces our mental state and inner mind. The art of being aware of our mind and thoughts will let us be more in tune with our own nature and know exactly why we do the things we do and let us be who we are and allow us to become introspective and examine each aspect of our life. We also will be able to control our thoughts and actions and become a more fulfilled happier successful person as a result. Knowing these details about our thoughts allows us to be more in tune and successful people in general.

Awareness of our intentions

Awareness of intent is an extremely important part of being aware human being in this world. We need to focus on our good intentions and having and harvesting good intentions rather than being extremely negative and wanting bad for others. Intent is an integral part of functioning in this universe. Most people are simply not fully aware of the intentions they hold for specific events outcomes or things in life. People live their lives in a state of lack of awareness. Most of the things they do they do with the concept of not possessing any level of awareness and usually within a state of a lack of oblivion. This is not the way you want to go about living your life. You will commit actions and deeds that you're completely unaware of that will or may cause harm to others unbeknownst to you.

Awareness of our present reality

We must be aware of our current reality and not live in a state of delusion, confusion, lack of understanding or knowing. For knowing what we're doing and where we are at in our lives allows us to exhibit traits of happy people and allows us to become closer to elevated states of bliss and happiness. It's important to be extremely aware of anything that we do in our lives and focus on the good aspects of our world. We must know what is happening to us and where our life is heading and how we feel on a daily and momentary basis. This allows us to be aware of our current reality and live in states of happiness and goodness. Awareness of anything that we partake in allows us to exist in elevated levels of happiness, joy, positivity, and begins a snowballing effect of more joy in our life and within our soul and being.

If you live in a state of awareness and harmony, you become fully aware of each and every deed that you commit and each and every thought that graces your mind and presence. You fully understand and comprehend why you commit the very actions that you do and it will become an integral part of yourself.

Existing in a state of awareness and harmony allows you to become a better person in general and grow your gifts and grow in happiness, love and light. You will become elevated and become a much happier person because there are many energies present within the concept of being self-aware, and energies will build upon themselves and create more harmony, peace, and bliss for you and those around you.

Chapter 11

ACHIEVE THE SUCCESS THAT YOU DESERVE

Success comes with great pride and hard work and goal setting and it's easy to be successful and accomplish your goals. You are a successful, wonderful accomplished amazing person. Being successful and happy isn't just a state of mind. It's something that is a way of life, and a way that people need to live and be when it comes to being a specific kind of person. A successful person lives their life with great meaning and seeks to do well in this world and hopes to succeed. You deserve to be the very best person you can be and to achieve all the desires and dreams you possess in life and to be the most successful person you can be.

Are you a successful person? Have you attempted to achieve or accomplish different goals in your life? Have you tried to be a success and try to accomplish things yet? Maybe have not achieved these specific accomplishments or tasks? It's OK because if you're asking yourself questions, you actually possess the knowledge of being a successful person. You actually have it in you to accomplish goals and understand the concept of goalsetting, which is a great thing to do.

Successful people have many different methods by which they stay and maintain their success and by which they end up doing great things and being this way for their triumph and work. A successful person lives their life with triumph and knows what they want out of life and goes for the things they desire in this world. They do not sit back and do nothing and are always in a state of being productive. Success is an important part of being a happy person for once you're in a state of being a success in life and in your world, you can become a happier person. Success breeds and creates happiness while being a happy person internally can create and breed and make a very successful person. Success isn't necessary for happiness and happiness isn't necessarily a necessity for success, but a happy person can make for a better successful person and can elevate levels of success within a person's life, profession, work and in all aspects of what a person is accomplishing.

Successful people work extremely hard to get where they're at, and they have various methods by which they accomplish these tasks and deeds. They have a dedicated and hard work ethic and they're very meticulous and tedious with the things that they do as far as what it takes to accomplish these specific types of goals.

Many successful people set goals for themselves and work hard to accomplish these goals. On top of that they never give up and continue aiming for an achieving their specific and various dreams. In order to be a success in this world you have to go by different rules and sets and standards that are different from others. You have to live by specific rules on this planet, rather than what other people say or do.

Susan might be an accomplished insurance professional, but she doesn't possess any form of internal happiness. She is in a constant state of misery and depression in her life and has many unresolved emotions she has had to deal with as an adult. If Susan was happy then her success would skyrocket, and she would be more productive and do more in her work and profession and would also be able to escalate her work and life based on a contagious form of joy. Her success would then elevate into other areas in her life and her confidence would grow and she would do well in many things she attempts to partake in.

Happiness can assist a person with being extremely successful and can elevate their levels of success and can elevate their life in many different forms. If you are a happy person, you will become more successful in life and if you are a successful person. Once you're successful and do well in life your confidence grows, and you are then less fearful and more confident to do other things and participate in tasks and goals you ordinarily wouldn't attempt or may be too scared to try to do.

Being an accomplished person and doing well and things, and that you have in life, including small tasks and large goals, can elevate your levels of happiness and make you more fulfilled and joyous person. it is important to strive to be successful and do well at anything that you do for this will assist you with becoming a happier person, and it will create an effect of allowing your success to skyrocket and allowing it to see-through in other areas in your life.

Success comes from internal satisfaction and fulfillment and believing in yourself and your wonderful abilities. You are a great person who deserves all the good success in the world and who harnesses the beauty within your own shell of self.

There are specific traits that successful people do possess. They possess these amazing traits that allow them to do well in all of their given talents and abilities and they are hardworking, enthusiastic, determined people who value these traits and who seek to exist in a world where they love to establish themselves as great people.

There are many habits of successful people that are helpful and effective when it comes to assisting them with the great abilities they have and the things they seek to do.

Successful people often share habits such as setting clear goals, maintaining a consistent routine, practicing self-discipline, prioritizing lifelong learning, and networking effectively. They also tend to manage their time well and focus on maintaining a positive mindset.

Confidence is an extremely important part of being a successful person and possess large amount of confidence. Increase your levels of success and happiness in your life. Growing your personal confidence and self-esteem will allow you to carefully become a more successful and happier person overall.

Steps to being a successful person

Elevating your confidence

Your confidence is a key movement within your life, and it's a good idea to be in a state where you are elevating or increasing your confidence levels within yourself. Make sure that your confidence levels are very high and that you believe in yourself and anything that you do, and that you are number one at everything you partake in.

This will build your confidence and allow you to become a successful wonderful person.

Accepting and loving yourself unconditionally

You will want to love yourself unconditionally no matter what and love anything that you partake in or do and accept yourself in order to be a successful person and always strive to do that which is moral or good or upstanding.

Elevating your personal and internal strength

It's imperative to elevate your personal and internal strengths in your life. Focus on all the good aspects in your life such as positive family, friends, co workers and those who are close to you. Focus on all the great material possessions you own as well. Use these things to utilize a greater personal strength within yourself.

Focusing on the positives in your life

Focus on the positive aspects in your life. You are a wonderful, beautiful special person who has many good blessings in your life and it's imperative that you focus on these things and learn to appreciate the small things that you hold and possess and not allow others to bring you down or make you feel inferior or lesser. Really learn to appreciate all the positives you have in your life.

Increasing your mental strength

Increase and grow your mental strength- your mental strength is of extreme importance and sometimes it's easy to be depressed, sad or feel anxiety or confusion. People also feel angry a lot of the time and it's a good idea to harness a strong and decent mental strength. Having a mental toughness will allow you to deal with life's challenges and issues and let you be a happier person overall.

Set achievable and realistic goals in life

Set achievable and decent goals for yourself in your life. Your world is important and only you have the ability to achieve these goals. Sometimes life can seem boring, repetitive, or not as interesting without having achievable goals so it's a great idea for you to harness goals and focus on achieving these goals. With goals, a person can be happier in general and be more fulfilled and feel they have a purpose in life and a sense of purpose.

Never settle for less always want the best for yourself

Never settle for less- always want the best for yourself. Just know that you deserve the very best in life and all the great and good things that you truly deserve. Never settle for what is lesser than others or that which isn't good enough for you. Always seek to want the best for yourself and know that you are deserving of the very best.

Strive to be number one in all that you do

Strive to be number one and the best in all that you do. Always seek to be the best that you can be and do well in anything that you do, for this will skyrocket your confidence and allow you to become confident in all other arenas in life and let you be the confident amazing person you were meant to be. You will gain an enormous amount of happiness from this.

Be a hard and dedicated worker

Be a dedicated and work hard in everything that you do. Your work is important and so are you. Never do less work or focus on being lazy, for people who are lazy lack happiness and other positive qualities. Be the happiest person you can be and be a dedicated hard work at your job, at school and in all things that you partake in. This will increase your happiness and levels of success. Work hard at all that you do and display dedication, perseverance and ambition in everything that you do. This will allow you to become an incredibly successful person and let you manifest success in your everyday life and allow you to connect your hard work to determination and dedication in every area in your life.

Increasing your levels of happiness

Increase your levels of happiness by taking advantage of any avenue you can. Hang out with friends, go to movies, theme parks, practice self-care, focus on all the positives in your life, develop your confidence levels and do what it takes for you to become a happier more confident you and a better person overall and in general. Happiness creates more happiness love and joy in a person's life and in their life's journey.

Success is not an easy strategy to take advantage of or to accomplish. Being a successful person takes hard work, good energy, determination and an incredibly positive attitude and work ethic. You can focus on being a person who exhibits these traits by being more in tune with yourself, exhibiting responsibility, determination, dedication and hard work in your life.

The success you deserve in life is sky high though a person may not always understand or believe this. You deserve the greatest successes in life and not just to remain in the same place you're at, but to grow and elevate yourself into someone higher and greater than you are now and who you are truly meant to be. You too can be the wonderful achiever like so many out there if you only strive to attain your goals and do the right thing and be a strong person and achieve the goals you set out for yourself.

Being a happy person is not always an easy feat to accomplish or live through. When we strive to be healthy and happy people within our core and souls, we learn to exhibit many different behaviors and how to practice many means of reaching this wonderful phase in our lives. In order to be able to reach these phases we will need immense amounts of compassion, love, positivity and goodness and learn how to drown out any forms of negativity, anger, fear and hatred that might be present within us.

There are many methods by which a person can achieve happiness, success, gain greater control of their lives, and live in a more fulfilled state than being in states of depression, angst, anger, confusion and places people may tend to be, rather than their natural positive state of goodness and love. It's imperative to utilize these different methods so one can become a better, happier person overall and not live in lower states of darkness and depression.

Learning to become love and light and harnessing and utilizing positive energies is also another means by which we can learn and practice how to become happier and more fulfilled people. There are many theories on what makes a happier person, but it is definitely known that focusing on positive concepts in your life will help turn around any negative ones and shifting your gear towards existing within the notion of self-love and good. You're on your way to becoming a healthier positive and fulfilled you who can do more in life and who has greater ideals regarding themselves.

www.ingramcontent.com/pod-product-compliance
Lightning Source LLC
LaVergne TN
LVHW012027060526
838201LV00061B/4491